Carol

Carol

Maybe I Do...Maybe I Don't

GALE A. BUCHANAN

Every marriage is a love story.

PALMETTO
P U B L I S H I N G
Charleston, SC
www.PalmettoPublishing.com

Hardcover ISBN: 979-8-8229-4156-4
Paperback ISBN: 979-8-8229-4157-1
eBook ISBN: 979-8-8229-4158-8
Audiobook ISBN: 979-8-8229-4159-5

Cover - Col. Buchanan and Carol at one of the military events held annually when he was serving as commandant of Alabama Military Academy.

Carol: Maybe I Do…Maybe I Don't is a beautiful memoir of a Southern lady who faced obstacles in her personal life but did not allow them to dictate her destiny.

Contents

Preface

EVERY MARRIAGE IS A LOVE STORY. THIS IS MINE.

This book is my effort to document some of my life, thoughts, activities, and experiences that I wish I could share with Carol—even though she died November 6, 2022. After we lived together for over fifty-two years, it would seem that I could have said everything I wanted to say, but there are so many things I would like to say once again. Even though I must have told her that I loved her thousands, maybe a million times, I would give almost anything to be able to tell her just once more, "I love you."

She must have expressed her love for me (well, sort of) an equal number of times. Perhaps a bit of insecurity on my part, but I always had just a twinge of "Do you *really* love me?" She always responded, "Maybe I do…maybe I don't." She would say this in a musical tone. I always interpreted her response as "Why do you ask such a silly question? You know I love you."

After Carol's death, I found in her Bible several poems that have totally convinced me her love for me was real. These poems were not included in a book of poetry that she wrote for our children. I quickly admit that none of the poems spell out my name (with one exception), and the originals were identified only by a small C in the upper right-hand corner of each page. But in my heart, I know she wrote these poems especially for me.

Writing this book has been exceedingly painful to realize my loss of Carol but also a phenomenal joy to reminisce about the many good times we shared.

In no way do I want to leave the impression that we had a perfect marriage. We shared many disagreements, but we never ever even thought of falling out of love. I hope others who may care to read about our love affair will reflect on their own relationship. My hope for those who read this book is that it will bring peace, love, joy, appreciation, and understanding for their spouse, whether living or deceased. I emphasize that the events, activities, and situations mentioned in this book are true and all details are as correct as possible.

I am greatly appreciative of Brad and Judy for critically reviewing this manuscript and for providing photos. Carol's brother Jim was also helpful in reviewing the manuscript. They were all helpful in getting things as correct as possible. These reviewers were especially helpful in remembering some of the details that I could not. I am especially appreciative of the review by our sister-in-law, author Mary Buchanan, and Beth Moore, our niece. Also, non–family members deserve special thanks for reading the manuscript from a different perspective. Leanne Chafin typed the manuscript but also served as a reviewer. Other close friends, including Jan and Steve McHargue, Lesa Cox, Frances Copeland, Anne Young, and Lydia McDaniel, offered guidance as well. I am immensely grateful for all reviews and the help of everyone who made this book possible.

Introduction

I have authored three books pertaining to agricultural research, a cookbook, and, as a coauthor, a book on leadership in agriculture. I've also written technical chapters for several books and many articles about a range of topics, as well as numerous science articles and scientific papers regarding the results of my research.

In sharing my love story with Carol, it has been difficult to capture both our emotions and the many things that occurred during our lives. I hope that others who read this book will find comfort in our story. In this book, I wish to share something about Carol and me but, more importantly, that the union of us is far greater than the sum of each of us as individuals.

Like every love story, ours has highs and lows, but in the end, together, our love withstood the tests. I know we helped each other. In 2015, I became Carol's caregiver when she lost the ability to use the left side of her body due to a stroke. I was able to help her for the remainder of her life. This support was easy for me and for the world to see. But Carol was equally supportive of me in many ways, especially when I was terminated from my first administrative job. The help, encouragement, and support she provided for me were not so easily recognized by those outside our immediate family. It was a very difficult time in my life. Carol was there for me constantly. She truly helped me make a new professional life. The bottom line is we tried to help each other as best we could to make each of our lives as whole as possible.

I will start with a bit about each of us, how we met, fell in love, and lived for over a half century as husband and wife. The reader should appreciate that this book was written from memory by an eighty-six-year-old man. I simply cannot vouch for the order of events and activities. However, my family has helped as much as they can. I can remember many of the details of various events, activities, and experiences we shared—just not the precise order, specific date, or some of the details. My reviewers were exceedingly helpful in providing many details mentioned in this book.

Another reason for writing this book was to have a means of incorporating some of Carol's poetry. To me, some of her poems are quite good. However, since I am a plant physiologist—weed scientist—I claim no expertise in the arts.

As one would expect, a book about a life together that covered over half a century could be quite long. Consequently, I have tried to include only a few of the events and activities that provide the basis for our love story.

Carol

Carol was the firstborn child of Jimmy and Dixie Jones. She was born on May 24, 1942, in Montgomery, Alabama. Eventually, there were four girls and one boy in her family. Her father was a musician. In his early years, he was involved in a range of musical genres. Jimmy Jones and Hank Williams both had separate radio shows at the same station in Montgomery, Alabama. Since their shows were consecutive, they had many opportunities to visit. While we don't know for sure, we suspect they might even have sung together on occasion. While Hank went on to stardom as a country music singer, Jimmy gravitated toward religious music.

After a career in the US Air Force during World War II, he became a minister of music, as well as education director for numerous churches throughout the southeastern US. Carol grew up as part of a church family.

Attending high school in Bastrop, Louisiana, Carol fell in love with a fellow student named Kenneth Slomosky. Apparently, her parents didn't approve of their relationship. To complicate matters, her family relocated to Mobile, Alabama, just prior to her senior year. While she never talked about Kenneth very much, I was aware of the pain of a first love. They kept in contact on an occasional basis. I truly believed she always loved Kenneth, but it never bothered me. While she might have loved Kenneth, I knew she was *in love* with me. I sent word to Kenneth via one of Carol's siblings of her death.

High school for Carol was not a particularly happy time. However, as always, she excelled in academics and enjoyed her favorite sport—volleyball. Also, she was a member of the pep squad.

After completing high school, Carol attended Judson College, a church-affiliated institution in Alabama. Attending church and church-related activities was part of her early life growing up in a Christian family.

She studied at Judson College, then attended a secretarial school, and very soon married. Her first husband, Jimmy Sciple, was a US Marine. She adapted to the life of a marine wife rather quickly and was deployed with him to a marine base in South Carolina. She soon gained employment as a secretary for a local church. It was not long before she became pregnant and gave birth to a wonderful baby girl, Judith (Judy) Marie.

After Jimmy's military service, they relocated to Opelika, Alabama. Carol secured employment as director of personnel for a sporting goods manufacturer owned by Fob James, who later became governor of Alabama.

Having never pried much into her private life, I am not knowledgeable of all the challenges she faced as a marine wife. However, I do know the marriage was not successful, leading to a divorce.

After the divorce, Carol secured a job at Auburn University. Her former husband eventually enrolled at Auburn University, where he completed his studies in architecture, and later established an architectural firm in Mobile, Alabama.

Carol was assigned as the personal secretary to a senior distinguished professor in the Department of Agronomy.

My first meeting with Carol occurred when the department head assigned her to type correspondence for me. Working for me was just added work for Carol, but she did not complain.

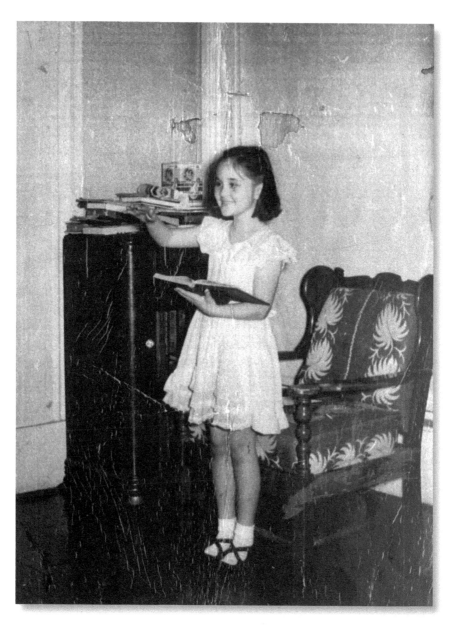

Carol at age ten. She is directing her imaginary choir.

Gale

I was the firstborn child of Joe and Lujette Buchanan. According to records, I arrived in this world on November 20, 1937, after my mother experienced an exceedingly difficult pregnancy and complications associated with a rural home delivery. Our home was out in the country in Madison County, Florida. From reputable sources, I was told that because of the complications with delivery, I was not given much of a chance to survive.

Apparently, most of the effort was directed at saving my mother, who was in critical condition. My father's baby sister, Jessie Clyde, who had just completed nursing school in Georgia, returned home and volunteered to stay and watch over my mother for an extended period. My dad always said that Jessie Clyde saved my mother's life. My parents eventually had four children—all boys.

My formative years were spent as part of a rural farm family with few noteworthy issues. As a member of such a family, I worked on the farm and attended the local school.

The first ten years were spent at the local school in Pinetta, Florida. For eleventh and twelfth grades, all students were transported to Madison High School, ten miles away in Madison, the county seat of Madison County. Being a very poor athlete, I never felt equal to most of my classmates. I did excel in academic studies, but that was poor consolation for a very poor athlete.

As a result of this situation, I was not a very active participant in the dating scene. My only foray in dating a city girl was a disaster. My father had arranged to leave the family truck so that I could use it for a date. After the date I would pick up my father at a local gas station and go home. It was a great plan—except for a small detail. The truck had been used to haul hogs to the market that day and had not been cleaned. The aroma was stifling. The city girl never complained. No more needs to be said.

The senior prom was a very special day in the life of high schoolers in the '50s, as it is today. I did have a date for the senior prom my senior year. She was Frances Stewart, now Frances Copeland, a sophomore still in school at Pinetta. She was also a close neighbor. While a sophomore, and only sixteen, she was the prettiest, indeed the most attractive, girl at the prom. Talk about boosting a person's morale! What a confidence builder! At the time, I didn't think much about getting her father to approve her going to the senior prom with me, especially with her being so young. Now, many years later, I think her father must have reasoned that I would take care of his daughter. In later years, her father would serve as a personal reference for me. One of my regrets was I never thanked her father for his faith in me.

After completing high school and working on the farm for the summer, I enrolled as a freshman at the University of Florida.

For the first time in my life, at the university, I felt as good as anybody. Being a student at, arguably, Florida's premier university made me feel equal to anybody. At the university everybody was equal—judgment was based on intellect, not whether you lived in town or the country. Nobody knew where you were from anyway. At the university, girls were the farthest things from my mind. Always working two jobs, and sometimes three, and studying in every spare moment left little time for anything else.

My first serious romantic relationship did not occur until late in my MS graduate program. During my last year of study for my masters, I started dating Kay Louise Unser, a French major from New Smyrna Beach, Florida. We really seemed to click. That is, until she embarked on a year's study at the Sorbonne in Paris, France.

This was a very trying time because I was in the process of making plans to continue studies for the PhD. At first, I was trying to get accepted into grad school at the University of California, Davis. After failing to secure an assistantship at Davis, I was accepted at Iowa State University in Ames, Iowa, graduate assistantship included.

Soon after my girlfriend Kay's departure and just before leaving for Iowa, I began dating another university acquaintance, Marcia Bartley. During the first year of doctoral studies, we began a correspondence leading to talk of marriage. And in the second year of studies, we were married. We lived in Ames while I continued in graduate school. Marcia was employed by the ISU Department of Agronomy, where I was an agronomy minor. Soon after I completed requirements for the PhD, we moved to Auburn, Alabama, where I took a job as an assistant professor at Auburn University. Soon after arriving at Auburn, Marcia gave birth to our wonderful daughter, Kimberleigh Jane. Marcia found employment as a secretary to the dean of engineering at Auburn. It was a great assignment and provided a stepping-stone for Marcia.

While the marriage appeared to be successful on the surface, something was apparently lacking. Consequently, Marcia filed for divorce after only seven and a half years of marriage. After the divorce, she relocated to Newberry, Florida. She then enrolled in the University of Florida, where she earned a master of education and a doctor of education. After completing her studies, she continued a successful career as an administrator in the Florida education system.

CHAPTER 1

The Beginning

SEARCH FOR A NEW MATE

For me, divorce was the first real major failure in my life. I thought I was totally to blame for the failed marriage. In fact, after over a half a century later, I guess my assessment was probably correct. I did not contribute in any meaningful way to strengthening our marriage. In any event, I liked the state of marriage, and while I thought our relationship was successful, apparently it was not, at least from Marcia's point of view. What I did learn from my first marriage was if ever given another opportunity at marriage, I would make it succeed—one way or another.

I made a commitment to myself to learn from my mistakes and do better the next time. I knew the first step was to select a person that totally shared my views, values, and philosophy of life. Most of the courtship with Marcia had been long distance while I was in Iowa. If we had spent more time together, perhaps we would have become better prepared to share a life together.

I embarked on finding the best mate for me. Not an easy assignment for a young professor striving to make tenure at a major university. My first attempts at dating were pretty much a disaster. My job as a research professor involved conducting research primarily at branch research stations located at various sites across the state of Alabama. Also, my major interest in research involved working in the fields, initiating experiments, collecting data, harvesting crops, et cetera. It also involved working with farmers and branch research station personnel. Not particularly fertile ground for meeting potential dating prospects.

One of my research colleagues, Tom Cope, and I were talking one day about research. He brought up my search for a new mate, which was pretty much common knowledge in the department. He mentioned that his former secretary, Carol Sciple, had worked for him after she left her previous assignment in the department. He related that she had relocated to Mobile, Alabama. This brought back memories for me as I recalled that Carol Sciple had been assigned to type correspondence for me. Her previous job in the department was as the secretary for Dr. Dana Sturkie, and she had simply been given the extra duty to type for the newest, young professor in the department. I recalled she was a no-nonsense professional who was extremely competent and did not waste time on gossip or engage in much small talk. I told Tom I would come to his office, where he could fill me in on Ms. Sciple. When I visited Tom, he said he didn't know much about her or her status but would share what he knew.

I continued to think about her as a possible partner and wanted further information. I asked Tom to tell me more. Seriously, it seemed like a genuine prospect. Tom really didn't know much more about her. He certainly knew nothing of her family. He did say one thing that I never forgot. He said, "I don't know if y'all are compatible and will hit it off." He further explained, "Her first husband liked to play ball, and you work all the time—so I'm not very optimistic." He just shook his head.

About the only real help Tom could give was that she was living in Mobile and staying with her parents. He also pointed out that her father was a preacher and worked at one of the big churches in Mobile. He made no distinction between minister of music and pulpit preacher. He also remembered that her father's family name was Jones.

Armed with this information, I knew I could track Carol down. Since it has now been over fifty years, I have forgotten many of the details, but some I don't forget. Basically, I remember making countless phone calls to churches in Mobile. These were the days before the smartphone, so I had a humongous telephone bill for that month.

I finally learned that a Jim Jones was a minister of music and director of education for Woodmont Baptist Church in Mobile. Great success! Getting the home phone number for Mr. Jones meant I was getting closer to contacting Carol.

I was beginning to make some progress. While I was a long way from finding my next wife, at least—maybe—I had the possibility of a prospect. I could think of at least twenty-five reasons not to place a call to Mr. Jones's home, but I knew I had to follow up immediately.

My next step was to place a call to the number for Mr. Jones and ask to speak to his daughter, Carol. At this time, I had absolutely no idea the age, temperament, attitude, or anything else of Mr. Jones. I knew nothing about his wife, his family, his dog, or anything else. In spite of all of the apprehension, I made the call. Again, age and lapsed time preclude me from remembering precisely who answered the telephone, but I know it was not Mr. Jones or his wife. Probably one of Carol's siblings answered the phone. I asked for her, and just like that, Carol was on the line. I was confident that if I ever got into a conversation with this Carol Sciple, I could take it from there.

After I told her who I was, of course she remembered me as the PhD who hadn't learned to write. I quickly followed up with my plans to be in the Mobile area in the next week or so and asked if she would like to have dinner with me. While I had not really planned to be in the Mobile area in the next week, I knew that it could certainly be arranged. I had several experiments at the research station in Fairhope (only a few miles from Mobile) and knew it was no problem to have some required travel soon, very soon.

To wrap up the call, I agreed to look at my schedule and see when I needed to be in the Mobile area to see some of my experiments. Then I would give her a call to alert her to a specific night for a date. This was a fine way to end the call. I was on cloud nine.

It happened to be springtime, when field experiments require attention. In coordinating with my technician, I sent him north to cover research at about four locations in that part of the state while I agreed to cover the experiments in the southern part of the state, particularly those closest to Mobile. Completing this coordination, issuing plans for my technician, and collecting supplies that I needed for my trip, I placed a call to Carol.

We readily settled on the day that I would be at the research station in Fairhope. We would go out the night that I would be arriving. I mentioned that, unfortunately, I would be traveling in a university work truck—the soil sample truck. It had a huge, mounted soil auger and really looked like a work truck. She responded very quickly, "No problem. We can use my car to go to dinner."

THE FIRST DATE

So far, all our conversations had been via the telephone. Now the first date was on the schedule. My first tasks were to plan for the research tasks to be accomplished and decide which experiments needed attention, what data needed to be taken, et cetera. Since that was my profession, that was no problem.

How to make a good impression on a girl was a bit more problematic. It had been several years since I had been on a date, not counting recent dating disasters, so this was no small task.

Carol had worked in the soil-testing laboratory for Dr. Cope for several months after she left Dr. Sturkie, and I had lost touch with her. Frankly, I had truly forgotten exactly how she looked. I remembered she was very short and small framed, with black hair. That was about it.

My first thoughts were how to dress appropriately. I selected my best pair of slacks and a blue striped shirt with button-down collar. Since it was spring and still cool outside, I decided to wear my favorite sweater, which I thought looked rather collegiate. Unfortunately, the temperature turned warm, and the sweater was absolutely not needed, but since it was part of an ensemble that I thought made me look my best, I wore it anyway. I later learned that her siblings laughed about me wearing a sweater when it was so warm outside.

As I approached her family's home, I started to panic. What did I forget? What did I overlook? Do I look OK? What do I say? How old was her daughter? Et cetera, et cetera, et cetera.

I laugh now for being so unsure of myself. I tried to park the obvious working man's truck so that it was at least not directly in front of the house. One last look in the rearview mirror and I headed for the front door. The door was opened by one of her siblings, but the first thing I saw was Judy, Carol's daughter, in pajamas leap from the floor to the back of the sofa in one great stride. It appeared she literally flew from the floor to the sofa. Then appeared Carol's mother and more siblings. We met and exchanged small talk, and then Carol's mother said that Carol would be in shortly.

I was not prepared for Carol's entrance. She was far more attractive than I had remembered or ever realized when she'd typed letters for me as a secretary. Not only was she beautiful, but her smile was absolutely beyond description.

After Carol told Judy to go to bed when Grandmother told her to, she said good night to everyone, and we were all alone. She had offered her car for our transportation since it was not appropriate to use a university work truck for personal convenience.

There were no awkward moments. We talked about family, work, likes, dislikes, world affairs, and everything else so easily. We discussed where to go to dinner. Since we both were knowledgeable about Mobile, we quickly agreed to head for the Causeway and see which restaurant we wanted to try. This was where many great restaurants were located. My favorite restaurant in this area was Palmers, but it catered to hungry working folks, not someone on a special date. So we selected a restaurant just a tad more appropriate for a first date and, I might add, considerably more expensive. Unfortunately, I don't remember the name of the restaurant, but it was the last restaurant on the Causeway before entering the tunnel.

It should be borne in mind that the point of a date was not necessarily to have a good evening—rather it was a part of a grand plan to find my next life partner. A lot was riding on this evening. This was what made the next issue more of a great concern.

After we entered the restaurant and were seated in a nice booth, the waitress gave us a menu. I knew the questions were coming, and I wanted to be prepared when the waiter came and asked for drinks. Carol was the daughter of a minister of music and education—really a preacher's daughter at one of the grand churches of Mobile. But the waitress appeared and asked for drinks, and Carol quickly said a glass of white wine. Whew! I was off the hook and didn't need to ask. I must have had a drink, but honestly, I can't recall what it was. I was so pleased that this had not turned into an awkward moment. We finally got around to ordering—seafood, of course—but we were talking so much, we hardly had time to eat. We finished dinner, still talking. Coffee, still talking. More coffee and more talking. We almost kept the table until closing time. After calls for unlimited coffee refills, I finally called for the check—still talking.

Without a doubt, by the end of the dinner, I had selected my life partner. Now the challenge was to convince Carol. But the date was not over. We got in the car, and I looked at the gas gauge; it was completely empty. I had some fun teasing Carol about using the oldest trick in the book—running out of gas on the first date. We got gas and headed home by midnight. Not bad for a first date. But we had not planned to sit out in front of the house and talk three more hours.

This was not a respectable time to bring a preacher's daughter home on the first date by anyone, university man or not. After taking Carol to the front door and leaving her to explain to her folks why she had stayed out so late, I got in my truck and left. Of course, we both had to work the next day. I had to be at the research station by 7 a.m. to meet the workers who had been designated and assigned to help me make weed counts and collect other data, and Carol had to be at her office at 8 a.m. But we were young and we could do it.

COURTSHIP

After our first date, there was absolutely no doubt in my mind I wanted Carol for my wife. But she did not express anything, of course; neither did I. I just knew. That made courtship pretty straightforward. We both wanted to learn about each other, including our dreams, hopes, fears, and everything else that it takes to make a life together.

We both had jobs. I was only five years out of grad school and trying to get established sufficiently to justify promotion to associate professor as well as earn tenure. She had an office job with a heavy construction company.

Much of my research effort was located at branch research stations scattered throughout the entire state of Alabama. In addition to a major station in Fairhope, just a few miles from Mobile, there were a number of other stations in the southern half of the state. I was pleased that my technician readily agreed to be responsible for experiments in the north while I was responsible for those in the south. Of course, this arrangement greatly facilitated courtship.

Very early in our courtship, Carol had to settle some business with her ex-husband in Anniston, Alabama. We scheduled her visit with me in Auburn rather than me going to Mobile. She was going to be in Auburn on a Saturday evening. Rather than scheduling dinner at a restaurant, I proposed to play chef and prepare a dinner that featured

Cornish Rock game hens and all the trimmings. Little did I realize that forty-five years later I would become a family chef, which led to one of my books, *Unexpected Chef.*

What a meal! The quality of the Cornish game hens was surpassed only by the quality of the company! While I had planned a very romantic evening, soon after dinner and a short period of small talk, Carol abruptly said she had to get on to Montgomery, where she planned to spend the evening with her aunt and uncle. We were both disappointed, but at the same time, we both knew it was certainly best to call it another perfect evening and plan for upcoming dates in Mobile.

In just a few short weeks, I was beginning to see I needed to concentrate my research in some stations in south Alabama. Also, I would probably need to visit at least one station almost every week. Monday, Tuesday, and Wednesday were always devoted to office work and coordinating with my students and technician and doing things that had to be done on campus, but then Thursday and Friday I was free to travel to the southern Alabama research stations.

By this time, in only a few short weeks, I had gotten to meet and know Carol's family and her favorite aunt and uncle as well. Carol had not met any of my family except my daughter. We knew we had to develop a plan to visit my folks as soon as possible. Together, we planned for her to come to Auburn on a Saturday morning. We could meet my family midway between the farm (Pinetta) and Auburn. She could stay with her aunt and uncle in Montgomery. I was able to get one of my brothers and his family to bring my parents to meet us midway between Auburn and the farm. We selected a seafood restaurant on Lake Blackshear just east of Americus, Georgia, for the meeting site.

The visit went extremely well. After introductions we all quickly engaged in friendly banter. The quite friendly atmosphere, along with a great seafood meal, made for a very successful visit with my folks.

By this time, I had wanted to tell Carol that I loved her, but I was quite reluctant to do so. No need to scare her off. One night as we were going to dinner, walking to the restaurant, totally unexpectedly and quite matter-of-factly Carol said, "You know that I love you." I responded very quickly that the feeling was certainly mutual because "I love you too." From that time on, discussion was never about if we wanted to get married. The discussion was only about when and where would be the best time to make the event happen. While our courtship lasted only about five months, we managed to get in about two years' worth of conversation. This, of course, enabled us to learn a great deal about each other.

We both agreed that the proper thing to do was tell both sets of parents first. Even though we were both divorced, we still maintained just a bit of innocence. As we both had been in failed marriages, telling our parents of our engagement was hardly necessary; it just seemed to be the proper thing to do. The simple action clearly reflected the values we both shared.

This called for a visit to both families quite soon. Since we had just visited my folks at Lake Blackshear, we thought we should tell her folks first. I was scheduled to visit Mobile the very next weekend.

I'm not sure whether it was that I had made a great impression and that they thought I was a good prospect or that they trusted the judgment of their daughter, but in any event, we had very positive feedback from her parents, who only wished us well. That took care of one set of parents; now for the second.

Auburn, the farm (my folks), and Mobile form a triangle that covers considerable mileage. It is about 225 miles from Auburn to Mobile, 305 miles from Mobile to the farm, and 220 miles from the farm to Auburn. The plan was for my daughter and me to meet Carol and Judy about midway between Mobile and the farm, and then we would get in my car for the remaining trip to the farm. We had such good support from her folks I didn't anticipate any problems with my folks. We arrived in time to attend church and had an absolutely fantastic visit. They gave their full blessings on our proposed marriage. It is not surprising that we received great support, encouragement, and best wishes from both of our families. What else could you expect for two firstborns who had already made up their minds?

PLANNING THE WEDDING

We both knew we had failed in our first marriages—one of the most sacred aspects of Christianity. We started out this marriage with no option for failure; this would be a successful marriage.

In view of our status and situation, we both knew we wanted to get married in a church. Maybe it would help make up for the failure to make our first marriage with other individuals work. So it was easy. We would ask the minister of Woodmont, where her father was the minister of music and education, to lead interference for us. It is quite true we were absolutely shocked when the minister said no. We were totally devastated. We knew that we had failed in our first marriages and were a divorced couple. We had sought forgiveness and were committed this time to making our marriage work. A follow-up request, but the answer was still a resounding "absolutely not in our church."

Carol's parents and family came to our rescue. We never thought anything more about the lack of support from the church proper, yet we received total support from her family as well as mine. Even though there might have been some reservations about this professor from Auburn, they could see that we were deeply in love and determined to marry.

Her father found a colleague in Whistler, Alabama, just north of Mobile, who agreed to be our minister and who would certainly perform the marriage.

As I had concentrated so much on the where, we had not yet set the date. By this time, it was late spring, and I had unbelievable commitments for my research and several technical meetings scheduled for the summer. It just looked like with all of my commitments, there just wasn't time for a wedding, let alone a honeymoon.

However, the scientific approach kicked in. Multitask! Why not combine a marriage (wedding ceremony) and honeymoon with some other event? The wedding would only take an afternoon, and then you could certainly do other things while you were on your honeymoon.

This made good sense to me. I'm not sure what Carol thought about it, but since we were so much in love, she agreed.

It just so happened that the First International Weed Science Conference had been scheduled for June. It was to be held at the University of California, Davis campus. Being aware of my work schedule as well as the International Weed Science Conference, it looked like we could get married early one week, then have the latter part of the week and weekend for a few days alone. Then we could spend the bulk of our honeymoon at the International Weed Science Conference in Davis. This sounded like a dream come true. Things were really coming together.

THE WEDDING

We scheduled a visit with the Mobile County officials to get our marriage license. No problem there. We were ready for the big day. The wedding ceremony was scheduled for late afternoon. Believe it or not, I spent the morning initiating an experiment on I-10, west of Mobile. As I indicated earlier, I was good at multitasking. Not bad getting a half day of research on your wedding day. It was an experiment in control of the horrible weed *Imperata cylindrica* (cogon grass). I still recall one of the herbicides I applied was dinoseb. I got some on me, and it turned my hands bright yellow. No matter how hard I washed, the yellow stain would not come off, so I got married with herbicide-stained hands.

We made it to the church in Whistler on time. But the minister was not on time. He had been fishing that morning and apparently had run overtime cleaning the fish. However, he finally arrived—still in his fishing clothes, but that didn't matter.

The only people present for the wedding were, of course, Carol and me, her folks, and the minister and his wife. While we were waiting for the minister, one of Carol's siblings entertained us by making bullfrog sounds. Carol might have made a few "ribbits" as well. Of course, this was a Jones trait!

On the drive back to Mobile, we were both in quite an introspective mood. For better or worse, we were husband and wife and all that that implies. We both knew we had made the commitment to each other for as long as we lived. For dinner that night, we were still in a reflective mood—yet we were extraordinarily happy.

LEAVING FOR THE WEED SCIENCE MEETINGS... ER, ER, ER, HONEYMOON

We were up early the next morning. The plan was to go by her folks' home to say goodbye to her family, then drive to the airport. We would leave our car at the airport, and the family would pick up my car later in the day and bring it back to the house.

What happened next was the saddest thing of the whole experience. As we said goodbye to the family and were getting into the car, Judy got in the back seat. She just knew she was going on the honeymoon. She couldn't believe that her mother and this new man would leave her alone with her grandma and grandpa while they were off to California. Unfortunately, we did just that.

We had a very short flight from Mobile to New Orleans and then were scheduled nonstop to San Francisco. Our layover in New Orleans was several hours. Near our departure gate was a pool hall. Carol suggested we shoot pool. I had tried it a few times previously without much success. Since the only pool hall in my hometown was also a beer joint, my parents didn't particularly relish the idea of a son going there for any reason.

But Carol broke the set and started pocketing balls. She must've gotten half the balls with the break before missing and giving me a turn. I watched intently as she was making shots that would have impressed the Hustler. I was beginning to wonder about this sweet Christian girl that I had just married. She then explained to me for the first time that she had played pool while in the hospital. She went on to explain it was not really a hospital but a center for severely depressed people. Part of her therapy had been to play pool. This was the first time that I was really aware that she had suffered severe depression in her life. Over the next few years, I learned a great deal about the seriousness of depression and how it affected Carol's life. Soon we heard the intercom announcing the boarding of our flight to San Francisco.

What a great time to visit San Francisco! Keep in mind this was 1970, well before the rampant crime, open drug use, and other undesirable aspects of our major cities such as San Francisco. We had a great few days exploring Chinatown, the wharf area, Telegraph Hill, and the famous trolley. And of course, learning more and more about each other and weeds!

The more time we spent with each other, the more I became convinced that we had made a great decision to marry. All too soon—way too soon—we had to check out of our wonderful hotel and head for Davis. Being a Scot, I said the Greyhound was probably the best way to get to Davis. Besides, it was only about ten or twelve blocks to the bus station. A bad, really bad decision. Of course, me being a world traveler, Carol offered no objections to this approach. Keep in mind this was before suitcases had learned to sprout wheels. The first three or four blocks went very well. However, by the eighth and ninth block, I sensed a bit of trouble. But the site of the bus station loomed in the distance, and our spirits were lifted. Trying to put the best spin possible, I exclaimed we were about there. Carol responded not too pleasantly, "It's about time."

I had compounded the problem. I'd made a poor decision by first taking the bus rather than renting a car and second by not taking a taxi from the hotel to the bus station. But all of these actions confirmed that marrying Carol was a great decision.

ON TO THE WEED SCIENCE
MEETING/HONEYMOON

In all of my travels as an academic, I had never gone by Greyhound. This was, indeed, a new low.

After purchasing two one-way tickets to Davis, we got a front seat so we could easily see the countryside. What a bus trip to Davis by Greyhound! The trip itself was worth a short novel.

Our driver was a new trainee named Carlos. The instructor sat on a stool right beside Carlos all the way and gave constant instructions.

While the scenery was interesting, the instructions to the trainee driver, Carlos, were even more interesting. It was a constant stream of recommendations and comments such as "now slow down," "apply light brakes," "do not pass," "watch that new car," "speed up," "slow down," "don't forget the signal," et cetera, et cetera, et cetera.

Carlos finally got us to Davis. In 1970, Davis was not the great university city it is today. There were two cabs waiting for passengers to exit the bus. Apparently, the only two passenger prospects were us. Both drivers aggressively claimed us as their passengers. Finally, *they* decided each would take one of us. You can imagine how that went over with me. Finally, I said we would go with the lady. End of discussion. We later learned the two drivers were kinfolk to each other. Welcome to Davis—1970.

We were very quickly whisked to the Voyager hotel—the conference hotel. If I had known the way and how close it was to the bus station, maybe we could have walked…not a chance!

THE FIRST INTERNATIONAL
WEED SCIENCE CONFERENCE

After checking in, we had a few hours to relax before the opening reception of the conference. I don't think Carol was prepared for the opening reception. Since the discipline of weed science is a fairly small one, I knew most of the weed scientists from the US who were in attendance. Also, I knew a number of foreign participants as well. I certainly knew just about all of the scientists present at the meeting from reading weed science literature. I took great pleasure in introducing my wife to friends and colleagues. Since they served heavy hors d'oeuvres at the reception, we didn't need dinner that evening, so we called it a night. We had to be up bright and early the next morning for a full day of the conference. We were scheduled for tours of Napa Valley to visit wineries and vineyards to see how weed science was involved in California's important wine industry. Carol could simply sleep in, lounge by the pool, take a nap, read a book, and just relax for the day.

When we woke the next morning, it was after nine o'clock. The 7 a.m. bus for the tour had long since departed. Carol was beside herself for making me miss the bus. I tried to tell her it was not her fault, as I was there too. I was not overly concerned. The first day was really just tours, and I had been to Napa Valley before. The technical conference didn't start until the next day.

After dressing and saying goodbye, I ambled down to the lobby area of the motel. Lo and behold, one of the conference hosts was just starting off to rejoin the group. He was traveling by car, so I quickly asked if I could ride with him. He graciously agreed. I got a personalized tour, and that was that. I called Carol to tell her the good news and said to have a great day and I would see her later that evening. All's well that ends well.

Most of my colleagues at the conference couldn't believe that I was spending our honeymoon at a meeting. While it might not sound like a great plan, I think a lot of men envied me!

I should point out that a part of my university job involved the responsibility for evaluating new herbicides developed by commercial companies. Consequently, I had many commercial contacts. I had a good friend whom I had worked with closely on a number of herbicides. He insisted on taking Carol and me to dinner. Our host, Philip Upchurch, a senior scientist with the Monsanto Company, was one of my industry contacts and colleagues. He was also a mentor and close friend. He had recruited me to work on a number of projects that he was involved in through some weed science organizations. One of the most important projects that I had become involved in was the popular publication *Weeds Today*. Upon Phil becoming president of the Weed Science Society, he appointed me to chair the *Weeds Today* project committee.

We readily accepted his invitation to dinner. He had selected the Firehouse Restaurant in Sacramento. Phil and I would work together in the herbicide area for much of the remainder of our professional life. He and I and a couple of other scientists also became involved in other projects as well. We were both founding directors of the Plant Growth Regulator Society. This was another spinoff of the Weed Science Society. The dinner and conversation were fantastic. Carol and I reminisced about that evening many times over the remainder of her life.

As the meeting drew to a close, we had hardly spent any of the money in our honeymoon account. Of course, I was on an expense account for the weed science meeting as well.

I suggested since we had not really had a true honeymoon, we take off a few more days and go to Lake Tahoe, which was only a couple of hours away. Great idea. We rented a car (no walking), got our airline tickets changed to give us another few days in California, and headed for Lake Tahoe. Again, we were alone, just the two of us in a great big world. We were really honeymooners now. Except for a bit of car trouble—we learned sometimes cars didn't perform as well at a high altitude such as that at Tahoe. The trip to Tahoe was a finishing touch to our honeymoon.

Returning the car to the San Francisco airport, we boarded a non-stop flight to New Orleans and then a short hop over to Mobile.

CHAPTER 2

Adjusting to Life as a Married Couple

BACK TO REALITY

Once we arrived back in Mobile as an old married couple, her family had a million questions. Subtly, her mother and father wanted to know "how it went." But they didn't really have to ask; you could easily see what we both felt. The next morning, we couldn't wait to load Carol and Judy's clothes along with other odds and ends in each of our cars.

I remember that both cars were quite full with hardly any room for Judy and the cats—Purdy and Freckles. Judy was to ride with Carol, and the cats rode with me.

Saying goodbye to the Joneses, we headed for the nearest gas station. Getting gas was no problem, but the cats escaped. Disaster. We looked for Purdy and Freckles for an hour or so. Carol finally just said, "Let's go and leave the cats," but I knew they were very, very important to her. Therefore, I was prepared to stay until sundown if needed. Fortunately, we found the felines, got them in the car, and we were off.

Arriving in Auburn after lunch, we proceeded to set up housekeeping. After unloading the cars, we started to get organized. The master bedroom was downstairs, while Judy's room was on the second floor upstairs. I immediately sensed her concern. This was a big change for Judy and Carol. While they were staying with their folks along with several siblings and pets in a small house, there was almost no room. Here they had a whole large house to rattle around in.

Since I had been out of the office for nearly two weeks, I had to get to work as soon as possible—like, the next day. Carol and Judy could continue setting up housekeeping while I was at work.

Getting back to the office was quite an experience. Everyone had many questions, especially the office secretarial staff. They had followed our courtship from day one. They felt they were a part of the whole process, especially since one of their former colleagues had married the youngest professor in the department.

After getting home, I made one of the stupidest decisions in our young marriage. My former wife and I had been one of four couples in a bridge group. We would meet once a month, with the host preparing dinner, then play bridge until usually after midnight. Carol so wanted to please me, she agreed to go even though she did not want to play bridge. To say it didn't go well is a gross understatement. We soon extricated ourselves from the bridge group. To this day I have not played another single hand of bridge.

Soon our first Christmas was approaching. Of course, both families expected us to visit during the holiday. Just as we had done when courting, we made the "mad triangle." We headed to Mobile and had a great couple of days with her family, then made the long journey from Mobile to the farm. After a couple of days with my folks, we headed back to Auburn. Fortunately, that was a short trip, only 220 miles, but we did get to see all the families and have a great first Christmas. Over our marriage we made the mad triangle several times.

My work at the university was going well. Phil Upchurch, the same man who had hosted us in Firehouse Restaurant in Sacramento, was the new president of the Weed Science Society of America. Since the *Weeds Today* project had been one of his earlier efforts, he wanted to make sure it succeeded, so he insisted that I become chair of *Weeds Today*. Eventually, I would become editor. I was already deeply involved in other professional projects for the society. This was just another project. My personal research effort was a full-time job. This was just extra work on my part. Involvement in *Weeds Today* would be part of many coming events and activities that affected my life as well as Carol's.

Since my boat was already loaded, Carol came to my rescue. She worked almost full-time on some of the many Weed Science Society projects that I had responsibility for.

Just before Christmas we learned that Carol was pregnant. After the first of the year, I found I needed to collaborate with one of my colleagues in Washington regarding *Weeds Today*. He was an employee of the USDA located in Beltsville, Maryland—just a few miles from DC. Even though Carol was now pregnant, she wanted to go with me to Washington. Since we were not on university business, I was on annual leave, and we drove. My host for the collaboration offered to let us stay with them while we worked on *Weeds Today*.

While we were working in his office in DC, Carol was to stay in Beltsville. After visiting with our host for a while, Carol decided that she wanted to see DC. Even though she was pregnant, she found a bus stop, figured out how to negotiate bus routes in the area, and headed to downtown. She spent the day visiting museums and galleries on the Mall. This was my first lesson in Carol's independence and willingness to do things that most people would be afraid to try.

We were becoming more and more comfortable with each other by this time. Carol quickly accepted the role of banker for the family. As

I handed over finances for the family, my only admonition was not to overlook paying the bills. To the best of my knowledge, for over fifty years, she never failed to pay a bill on time. In addition, she balanced the checkbook to the penny every month—something that I never even attempted.

After New Year's of our first year, we both agreed my job was to make money, and her job was to spend it wisely. Over half a century, that process worked well for us.

Little did we know the next big event in our life was about to unfold.

ALONG CAME BRAD

It was April and approaching the first anniversary of our marriage. Carol was in the last trimester of pregnancy, and I was going ninety miles an hour initiating new experiments literally all over the state. I was working, at the time, at the Tennessee Valley Experiment Station, only a few miles from the Tennessee–Alabama state line. One morning the station office received a message from a family friend. This was before cell phones. The message was "your wife is in the hospital." I knew the baby was not due just yet, so what was the problem? I did not take time to chase down someone on the telephone. I simply told the workers to clean up my sprayer and secure all the supplies and that I would be back as soon as I could. My plan was to take care of whatever the problem was and return as quickly as possible. Within minutes I had the big Ford work truck humming south.

When I reached Pell City, which is about the halfway point, I was hungry, but I didn't want to stop. Finally, I got a hamburger and a Coke, climbed back in the truck, and ate on the way. I went straight to the hospital in Opelika. I quickly learned my son had been born earlier in the day—a couple of months premature. He was fine but in an incubator. Carol was also doing well. I simply wanted to see her. Brad is now fifty-two years old. Knowing his temperament, I have no doubt he decided it was time to be born and simply made his way out. Also, knowing Carol, she undoubtedly agreed.

In a day or so, I brought Carol home. Brad stayed at the hospital for several weeks. This allowed Carol and me to get our lives back to something near normal. Soon we were able to retrieve Brad from the hospital and bring him home. Our world has never been the same since he joined us. The nursery, Brad's room, was across the hall from Judy's room. After a year Judy still demanded that I sit on the stairs until she drifted off to sleep. I spent many, many hours sitting at the top of the stairs waiting for Judy to go to sleep.

Carol now had plenty to do. Keeping house and taking care of a baby was a full-time job. Also, Carol was suffering from postpartum depression. By the time we brought Brad home, she was doing better.

Surviving depression was challenging enough, but about this time Carol was diagnosed with diabetes. Consequently, she was placed on insulin. This required pricking her finger to measure blood glucose levels, then injecting the prescribed insulin dose. These tasks are just aggravation for most diabetics. However, for Carol, they were exceedingly difficult. She suffered from severe trypanophobia (fear of needles), making each finger prick and injection of insulin a rather traumatic experience. In fact, many years later she suffered a stroke in that part of her brain commonly associated with diabetes.

ACCEPTING A HUSBAND WITH NO MECHANICAL SKILLS

Soon after we were married, Carol had to learn about my seemingly total lack of mechanical skills. This was such a shock because her father had about every tool you could imagine, and he knew how to use them. Her father could fix almost anything, from a radio in the old days to any household appliance to the automobile. Carol assumed that since I was a man, I should be as adept at using tools as her father. Unfortunately, she didn't realize the tremendous deficiency in the Buchanan family. Most Buchanans have trouble even playing a radio, let alone fixing one.

Fortunately, Brad inherited all the mechanical skills from the Jones side of the family. He has a wonderful tool set and can fix just about anything imaginable. He makes up for my total lack of mechanical skills with his unique ability to fix or work on just about anything.

Carol spent many years trying to get me proficient in fixing things. She bought numerous books on how to fix anything. She really tried to encourage and make me a handyman. It didn't work. I don't think Carol ever came to terms with the fact that I was just not handy. My only success was in keeping an up-to-date telephone list of reliable repairmen and businesses.

HIJACKING

By the time of our second Christmas, we were truly a family. As 1972 dawned, little did we know what a challenging year it would be. I was devoting an unbelievable amount of time to the popular magazine *Weeds Today* as well as serving on the editorial board of the technical scientific journal *Weed Science*. I had been manager of ad sales, chairman of the board, and now editor in chief. As editor, I had to secure copy from weed scientists around the US and Canada and then prepare all copy and ensure we had adequate ad revenue to pay for the layout, printing, and mailing of each issue.

To finalize each issue, I flew to Memphis, Tennessee, to work with the printer. Late in the afternoon of November 10, 1972, I left the printer with a paste-up copy of the fall issue of *Weeds Today* and headed for the airport in Memphis. It was a short flight from Memphis to Montgomery, with one stop in Birmingham. That brief stop turned into a three-day odyssey. The plane was to arrive in Montgomery at about 5:00 p.m. I'd be home by 6:00 p.m., expecting Don and Mitzi Gates to be our guests for dinner that evening at 7:00 p.m. Great plan, but three gentlemen from Detroit had other ideas. We were hijacked as we were about to take off from the airport in Birmingham.

There were sufficient experiences and excitement over the next three days to last a lifetime. I won't go into any of the details about the hijacking here but invite the readers to pick up a copy of the book *Odyssey of Terror* by Ed Blair to read the full story. Also, *Reader's Digest* (May 1973) has an article by Joe Blank that also provides many details regarding the hijacking, including his interview with me.

As one could imagine, Carol had been bombarded with calls from the media. She turned all the calls down, with one exception. As soon as we were able to return from Montgomery, she told me she had agreed for me to be interviewed by a single reporter from the *Birmingham News*.

This reporter came to our house as soon as we returned from the airport for the interview. The reporter got a good story, and I had the opportunity to share all my thoughts and ideas regarding the hijacking. We finally got to bed well after midnight. I had to get up early the next morning to catch a flight to London. I was scheduled to attend and participate in the British Weed Science Conference in Brighton, England, on Tuesday.

Some might find it hard to believe that after such a hijacking experience and returning home late Sunday evening, I would leave at 5 a.m. the next day for a weed science conference in England. But for well over half a century, Carol never once complained about my work schedule. What a blessing!

WHAT'S MY LINE?

The office was bombarded with questions about the Auburn professor who was involved in the hijacking, but the office staff could truthfully say, "He is not available."

The hijacking experience pretty much defined 1972. In early 1973, I got a call from New York. The person verified who I was and asked if I would consider being on the show *What's My Line?* I told the caller I was very busy; I would have to look at my schedule and get back to them. I really didn't want to take time to go on any TV show. It seemed like such a frivolous activity for someone who had serious work to do. So I consulted with Carol. She thought the matter over and thought it interesting. She reasoned it would give my discipline of weed science some recognition.

Carol strongly encouraged me to call and accept the invitation. So the next day I called the person back and accepted the invitation to appear on *What's My Line?* The taping was scheduled for some time a month or so later. They said they would provide tickets and pay all expenses. It would be of no cost to me, though there was no monetary compensation paid to the contestants. In a few days, we received the show tickets and plane reservations for Carol, Brad, and me, so we were off to New York. Brad was now almost two years old—walking well, indeed, running everywhere.

We flew first from Columbus, Georgia, to Atlanta, then from Atlanta to Washington Dulles and then on to New York, LaGuardia. They had us booked into the Waldorf-Astoria hotel. Our host took us for a couple of great meals and made sure that we were well taken care of. During some free time, Carol and I were exploring the lobby area and shops in the Waldorf, and somehow Brad and I got separated from Carol. Brad needed a diaper change. He promptly kicked off his wet diaper and dashed across the lobby of the Waldorf to Carol, who was on the far side. He had absolutely no clothes on except for a very small shirt. Of course, all the employees at the front desk as well as other people in the lobby got a great charge out of seeing a naked little boy running across the lobby of the Waldorf-Astoria.

Taking care of Brad kept Carol from seeing the show taping, and she was out of the country when it was aired on TV. This was in the days before shows were archived, so Carol never saw the show. My line was that I was a weed scientist. Soupy Sales would never have guessed it. However, Arlene Francis got it in only a few minutes with a few very specific questions. Finally, the hijacking experience was put to bed.

CAROL EXPANDS HER HORIZONS IN THEATER

Carol's mind was never still. It seems she was always planning something. Of course, I never knew what exactly she was thinking. I do know she wanted to experience new things. Consequently, she often wanted to take advantage of university opportunities.

Her first venture into taking courses at Auburn was a course in the general sciences—earth science. It was exciting and influenced her to start thinking about our world. She was doing well—so well in fact that I thought she might declare a major in a science area. But she soon started to talk about other areas within the university. She talked about how exciting it would be to take a course in theater.

The next quarter she enrolled in a beginning course in theater. Oh, how excited she was. Many of her classmates constantly talked about the theater productions for the coming season. The first production was *The Prime of Miss Jean Brodie*. Carol was interested and wanted to be in the production. She got a copy of the play and, after studying intently, decided she wanted the lead. Unfortunately, she did not land the lead role. She did land a good role as Sister Helena, a nun. Believe it or not, she developed a British accent such that it sounded like she was from the Old World. She threw herself into the production as much as any student possibly could and, I might add, gave a convincing and successful performance as Sister Helena.

The main production for the season was *Cabaret*. Again, Carol was so excited. She set her heart on the lead role in *Cabaret*—the Sally Bowles role. If I could have made it happen, I would certainly have given her the part.

Again, Carol did not get the lead role, but she did get a quite different role than she had had in *The Prime of Miss Jean Brodie*. She was to play a role as a prostitute. It allowed her to play a very different role from that of Sister Helena. I always teased her about turning from a nun to a prostitute in one season.

Carol as nun Helena as she appeared in the play
The Prime of Miss Jean Brodie. While it cannot be shown,
she developed a British accent that sounded really authentic.

Carol was a real trouper. Students didn't just get to have roles in plays—they had to design and build sets, using hammers, saws, nails, and screws. They learned theater from the ground up.

After the production of *Cabaret* and its successful run on campus, Carol and a guest (me) were invited to the cast party. What a party! I soon noticed none of the key theater faculty were in attendance. I was the only professor at the party. Of course, I was only the guest of one of the cast members.

As the evening wore on, the party got progressively rowdier. We were in someone's large house. I noticed that some of the rooms were watched very carefully. Finally, Carol shared with me that some of the cast members were smoking marijuana. I almost panicked. Carol was much calmer. Since it was after midnight, we finally found the host, expressed our appreciation for being invited to the party and our regrets for leaving so early, then made a hasty exit. Fortunately, I escaped without any incident. No one ever knew that I, the young agronomy professor, had attended such a party.

I fully expected Carol to be eager to sign up for theater the next year, but following tradition, Carol decided she wanted to take courses in Italian opera. And she did.

CAROL'S TRIP TO THE MIDDLE EAST AND RUSSIA

For five years our marriage and life were going very well, although Carol's depression was often very challenging at times. She was now seeing a doctor regularly. It seemed she was prescribed a new antidepressant quite frequently. I finally learned that many of these antidepressants had side effects about as serious as the depression itself.

Carol learned that a church group from Anniston, Alabama, was planning a trip to the Holy Land and other places. She expressed to me it had always been a life dream to visit the Holy Land. I strongly, no, very strongly, encouraged her to pursue such a trip. She fretted about finances, and taking care of Brad, and everything else. I surmised that such a trip might be therapeutic. Quite frankly, I believe she changed her mind about going at least ten times before she was required to put her money down. Even after she had committed and planned to go, she changed her mind a couple more times. But I was equally insistent that this was a good idea, and sure enough, when the day finally came to leave, she was packed and joined the group. From my perspective, I think she enjoyed the trip. I think it was some of the best use of money we ever spent.

I'm proud of how our whole family worked together to make it all happen. Her aunt and uncle came over from Montgomery and spent the entire two weeks in the house taking care of Brad and Judy. Consequently, I did not miss a single day at work, including some National Guard assignments. Carol had countless stories to tell when she returned. While I did much of the traveling, especially internationally, she now had stories to tell about places I had never been, such as the Holy Land and Russia, Lebanon, and Syria. We could compare notes on Russia, but she saw parts that I didn't get to see. She always enjoyed relating some of her experiences in the Holy Land, Lebanon, and Syria.

I never forgot the night she returned to Columbus, Georgia. I was coming home from the National Guard summer camp at Fort Rucker (now Fort Novosel) just south of Columbus. After meeting her at the Columbus airport, we decided to stay in Columbus for the night. We talked most of the night until the wee hours of the morning. I'd never seen her so excited and happy all at the same time, but it was great to have her home again. We slept until almost nine the next morning, then headed home to see the children. They had survived the two weeks with no problems at all.

A NEW HOUSE

Carol never said a word about our house, but deep down I knew, and she knew, that she had not picked it out. I came home from work one day, and she said she wanted to show me something. It was a house on Cary Drive—the best address in Auburn. I expressed little interest until she showed me that she had worked out all the details. She only needed my signature and approval. How could I not support her plan? It was almost a dream house for a middle-class family. It was situated on three lots in Cary Woods, with the main house over four thousand square feet. In addition, there was an apartment attached to the house above the garage, a two-thousand-square-foot recreational house, and a storage house also on the property.

The main house and apartment had solid oak floors throughout and solid black walnut paneling for the dining area. There were so many closets and storage areas I don't think we ever filled all of them, even after several years of living in the house. The house had been built by a contractor, so everything was custom designed. The one thing lacking was the house had never been landscaped—not a single ornamental plant had been planted around the house. This was certainly no problem because I enjoyed taking care of that small detail. The price was right, and the offer on our existing house was acceptable. I think having a home that Carol had selected boosted her morale. Of course, interest rates were sky high at the time of the deal, but why sweat the details?

The move was a pleasure. Leaving Pick Woods and heading for Cary Woods was frankly quite exciting. Judy was ecstatic she had her own apartment far away from her parents, and that gave her a sense of independence. She certainly didn't want me sitting at the top of the stairs until she drifted off to sleep. Even though the apartment was attached to the house, it was almost on another street. While we were still moving into the new house trying to get settled, another opportunity manifested itself.

HAWAII—THE FIRST TIME

One of my industry collaborators had announced a meeting in Hawaii that included spouses. Carol and I were invited to attend. All I had to do was write a short presentation. Of course, such conferences as these were not official university business, so I had to take annual leave. I was not on an expense account. Expenses were paid by the industry. Such trips usually were only for researchers; however, this sounded more like a vacation.

On the flight to Hawaii, we had a several-hour layover in Las Vegas. Carol was intrigued by the slot machines in the airport, so I encouraged her to try her luck. She won several dollars and was so excited, and I encouraged her to keep playing. She had wanted to pocket her winnings, but since I urged her to keep playing, soon all of her winnings were gone. I don't think she ever forgave me for that.

One day during the conference, the scientists were scheduled to see some Hawaiian agriculture while spouses were scheduled to go on a shopping spree. This didn't appeal to Carol, so she insisted that she be included on the ag tour rather than going shopping. She won the day and stayed with the scientist group instead of the ladies who went shopping. I think Carol made a wise choice seeing up close how macadamias, mandarins, coffee, papaya, and other exotic fruits and nuts are produced.

CHAPTER 3

Becoming a Family

FAMILY TRIPS AND VACATIONS

In the first decade of our marriage, we took quite modest family vacations. Usually, our family would only take a couple of days and head to the beach, usually Gulf Shores, Alabama.

We soon learned that Washington, DC, was a very inexpensive vacation—when we did it our way. We would drive to DC, getting a couple of meals and gas on the way. We stayed in Northern Virginia, where motel rates were quite reasonable. That was before the days of the Metro, but there was an excellent bus system that would take you to downtown DC for just a few dimes. Museums and art galleries were free, and the only expense for the day was a hot dog and Coke for lunch. Back in the motel, bologna sandwiches and Cokes sufficed for dinner, and cereal and doughnuts for breakfast the next day. What a vacation!

An occurrence on our first vacation visit to Washington, DC, provided the basis for many laughs for our family over the years—at Judy's expense. We had driven all day and finally got through Richmond. Now it was only one hundred miles to DC, and Carol and I started discussing where we should stop for the night. We wanted to be close enough to DC where there would be bus service to downtown. Judy, who was seated in the back seat with the other children, pointedly asked, "When are we going to cross the Mississippi River and see the Grand Canyon?" She thought we were going to Washington state. A reasonable assumption for a smart ten-year-old kid—if no one bothered to inform them exactly where we were going!

To add another laugh, Carol chimed in, "We will be in DC when we cross the Pot-O-Mack."

Then there was the famous golf vacation. Carol had the idea of really learning to play golf. She and the children went to the local Auburn country club and took golf lessons so they would have fundamental skills. We bought golf clubs and planned our vacation, which we dubbed The Golf Vacation. We selected Gulf Shores, Alabama, as the site. There were plenty of municipal golf courses in the area, and of course, the beach was always good, and who complained about the opportunities for seafood meals? Just what could go wrong? You guessed it! When traveling to south Alabama in the summertime, expect rain and more rain. We tried and tried. Rain is not good for golf or the beach for that matter, but a family can still enjoy seafood despite the weather. So all was not lost.

Another complication that contributed to our disastrous "golfing vacation" was Carol somehow managed to break a bone in her ankle. This immobilized Carol almost completely.

These inconveniences didn't dampen our desire to golf! Several weeks after returning from vacation, Carol and I took off one Saturday to go to Callaway Gardens, located in Pine Mountain, Georgia, which has a beautiful golf course, and try our luck again. We paid the fees, disdaining a cart because we thought we would enjoy the exercise. We were off to play golf. On about the third or fourth hole, Carol overshot the green, and her ball had a horrible lie. She was on the other side of the green while I was on the side where her ball landed, so I proceeded to help her with her lie. I had assumed that she could not see what I was doing, but unfortunately, I was wrong. She was furious that I had moved her ball. She said, "We are going home. I do not want to play golf anymore." I responded that we had already paid for thirty-six holes of golf, eighteen for her and eighteen for me, and it just didn't make sense to quit and go home. Oh yes, we can go home, and just like that our golfing career had ended.

For years after, any time Carol felt low, which was more and more frequently, she said, "I'm going to sell my golf clubs." I was just as adamant and stubborn, and I responded, "You are not going to sell your golf clubs." So we kept her golf clubs in the attic next to mine for the next forty-five years. In 2023, a year after Carol's death, we gave her golf clubs to Combine Ministries Thrift Store in the hopes that they bring joy and peace to someone else. Golf certainly didn't bring us any closer together.

We went to several different venues for family vacation. One year we took on Florida, including Silver Springs, St. Augustine, and other sites in central Florida. One year we took a trip to Disney World. It seemed we always went at the hottest time of the year. I still recall Space Mountain soon after it opened. I was expecting a science-based ride that would be educational. Unfortunately, I learned too late it was nothing but a horrible roller coaster—*in the dark*. The only benefit from this vacation experience was the cool boat ride in It's a Small World. One year we visited Tennessee (Gatlinburg) and Lookout Mountain (Chattanooga) for a different experience.

Another year we traveled to Pennsylvania Dutch and Amish country, including Gettysburg. I still recall we were driving through the Gettysburg National Cemetery seeing some of the monuments when Carol began to notice that most of the monuments were for units of the Union Army. "Where are the monuments to the South?" she asked. I pointed out this was a USA cemetery. The "losers" don't get much visibility. Carol replied, "We've seen enough. Let's go home." So, just like that, we exited in the middle of the drive through Gettysburg National Cemetery and set a course for Auburn, Alabama—never looking back and never returning.

BIRTHDAYS

Birthdays were always a very special time for Carol. Many times, she expressed to me that she had often cried on her birthdays when she was young because she would never be that age again. Most people don't give birthdays a second thought. But these would be special days for Carol. She always wanted to make them something special for the children and me. She was equally adamant that she wanted no special things done for herself. One of my regrets is that I never ignored her wishes and hosted a big blowout just for her.

For example, one of Brad's birthdays, she contracted with a pilot at the local airport to take the guests and Brad up for a short flight. They would fly over each guest's house. Of course, they had to make multiple trips. What a birthday party for Brad and his friends!

Another time for Brad's birthday, Carol went to the animal science department and found a couple of real cowboys that could do rope tricks. This was also a hit with the boys.

For Judy, birthdays were more traditional. Usually they involved friends for a sleepover, usually with a Hershey bar pie.

I was not left out when it came to birthdays. One year I returned home for a birthday dinner, and Carol met me at the door explaining my birthday present was in the bathroom. Knowing Carol, I did not know what to expect. I certainly had no idea why a birthday present should be located in the bathroom, but anyway, I went into the bathroom. My birthday present was in the bathtub, which was completely full of water, with six giant catfish swimming around. I recalled sometime earlier I had mentioned the importance of catfish being really fresh. So she had gotten me probably the freshest catfish that you can get—live ones.

I will never forget the birthday bed-and-breakfast in Thomasville, Georgia. Quite an unusual experience, since Thomasville was only a few minutes away from our home. We made like we were tourists just visiting the South. The proprietor was not fooled a minute. She was a retired army colonel and quickly found out I was a colonel and lived only a few minutes away. The conversation with the colonel was exceedingly interesting and the food even better. A birthday I'll never forget!

CHAPERONE FOR A BAND TRIP

Brad was a member of the Auburn High School Marching Band. In view of this, we always saw the first half of the football games, watched the band, and promptly headed for home. During his senior year, the band planned a trip to Europe. They were scheduled to visit a number of countries, including Austria, Switzerland, Germany, and France.

Somehow Carol was recruited to be a chaperone for the tour. For this trip, there were never any second thoughts about going. Carol was determined to make this trip special for her son. To round out the trip, Carol invited her favorite niece, Beth, my brother's daughter, to accompany them.

Apparently, the trip was a great success. However, there were two noteworthy occurrences that I'll share. First, a bit of background. Beth and her family often vacationed in North Georgia in a little town called Helen. This town is located in the lower foothills of the Appalachian Mountain chain. We in South Georgia generally referred to this area as the Georgia Mountains—at least, the terrain isn't as flat as it is in South Georgia. Helen has a German flavor.

Anyway, according to Carol, the first morning in Switzerland, Beth came down for breakfast. For the first time since arriving, now, in the daylight, they had a great view of the Swiss Alps in the brilliant morning sun. As soon as Beth saw the mountains, she explained they were just like the Georgia Mountains. Carol told that tale many times over the years—how Beth compared the Swiss Alps to the North Georgia foothills.

The other story about this trip involved me. It just so happened that when Carol, Brad, and Beth left for Europe, I left for the Republic of Korea (South Korea). I had two weeks of military duty. Frankly, I got to feeling a bit low toward the end of the second week of the conference. My family wasn't home, and I was on the other side of the planet. I also suspected that Carol was feeling the same while trying to keep up with all the band members as they journeyed across Europe.

What does a caring husband do? Of course, he makes a call to his wife to cheer her up and make himself feel better as well. Sounded like a great idea, and I couldn't wait to put it into play. Not so fast, Buster.

First, what time to call? Figuring out what time to call was not an easy matter. Keep in mind Switzerland is about seven or eight hours east of our home in Alabama, and I was about twelve or thirteen hours west of our home. That was west of the international date line. I'm sure for some people this would have been a very easy calculation, but for me it was very confusing.

Now that this was figured out, I calculated that the best time to call would be between nine o'clock and ten o'clock in the evening, Carol's time. This would give her time to complete the day, eat dinner, and get settled in the room for the evening. I can't remember what time it was for me, but it was a time when I was off duty.

The next problem was where do you go to make such a call? I first tried the military. It was a snap to make overseas calls in the military as long as it was on official business. Of course, this was not official business. I had to start looking elsewhere.

Soon I learned that there was a "call center" in Seoul. From the call center, you could make calls to anywhere on the planet. I finally got the address of the call center and after a couple of cab rides got to the center. The ideal time to call was rapidly approaching. I assumed that it would be a snap to make the call once I got in the call center. How wrong I was. The procedures, I'm sure, were quite simple for a native Korean, especially one who had a PhD as well as training in the law. But I finally figured that out. Now it was well past my ideal time to call. At least I was making progress. Around Carol's midnight I was awarded a line that I was later told was quick for a line to Europe. But I surmised that Carol would answer the phone, have a sweet but brief conversation with me, and then could roll over and go back to sleep. So no harm was to be done. It seemed like an elegant plan.

Now that I had my line, I dialed the number of the lodge where they were staying. The gentleman who picked up the phone was obviously in a deep sleep, but he was finally roused enough to answer. Unfortunately, he hardly spoke any English. For the first time, I sensed real trouble. Finally, I got through that I wanted to speak with one of the guests. I spelled out C-A-R-O-L B-U-C-H-A-N-A-N. I think he finally comprehended and, checking his roster, found that he did have a Carol Buchanan registered at the lodge. Now we were getting somewhere.

He finally got across to me that he understood and would go fetch this Carol for the phone call. That comment puzzled me. Why not just ring the room? I later learned this was a lodge with many small, very small, cabins scattered over the Swiss mountainside, with no phone service to the cabins.

A dozen times while he was gone, I started to hang up, but I knew that I was in too deep to terminate the call. So I waited. By now, no matter how great my idea and intent were, I knew that I was in trouble and had made a monumental error in judgment.

I don't think Carol really appreciated what I had gone through to get her on the line. Over the years, Carol and I had many great phone calls with each other. I can assure you that this was not one of them. I won't say more.

DARK DAYS OF DEPRESSION

While I have never suffered from depression, I have learned a few things by living with someone who did suffer from this medical condition. For several years, bouts of depression would descend on Carol and then vanish just about as quickly as they had begun. After about a decade into our marriage, Carol went into a particularly dark period. She was now seeing a doctor regularly. He suggested she check into a clinic for a few days (weeks) in a nearby city, Columbus, Georgia. He also recommended that I participate in some of the sessions with her. Of course, I quickly agreed.

I think I got more out of the sessions than did Carol. The doctor caused me to think that I could help by better understanding how depression affects people. After a period, Carol started to talk. I asked, "What would you like to do?" She responded that she would like to take a trip. I had plenty of Delta airline points, so we could go anyplace Delta could take us. To this day I never knew why she picked Vancouver, British Columbia, but that's exactly where she wanted to go. As soon as she was discharged, we got tickets to Vancouver and spent three wonderful days there.

We didn't find many tourist attractions. We enjoyed just exploring the beautiful city. They do have some very fine restaurants. We spent some time in a beautiful park and thoroughly enjoyed the trip.

A few years later, after Carol experienced another episode of depression, we again took another trip, this time again to the northwest US. I was very much part of the planning, because I had always wanted to visit Seattle. After we talked about that possibility, Carol was game for a trip to Seattle.

Visiting the fish market was worth the whole trip. Just watching one of those people sail big fish across several rows of counters only to be caught by another fish catcher was an experience I'll never forget. Now that it has been many years, I wonder if the fish market with the fish-throwing team is still available for the public to see. I'd like to see it once more.

We also took a boat ride to an island. I can't remember the details or the name of the island, but it was very interesting. In all our travels, we always looked forward to taking a boat ride—London, New Orleans, Paris, Boston, Seattle, and some more I can't remember.

We just happened to be visiting Seattle at the time of the annual Bumbershoot. We asked several people—what is a Bumbershoot? It took a while, but we finally got the answer. Apparently, *bumber* is a modification of the umbr- in *umbrella*, and *shoot* is an alteration of the chute in *parachute* (since an open parachute looks a little like an umbrella). Carol and I just called the event the umbrella event. But it was a great experience. The Bumbershoot, along with the Space Needle and fish market, made for a great holiday. Our trip to Seattle was a very enjoyable experience and I think really helped Carol get back to a sense of normalcy.

ANYBODY WANT TO JOIN THE NAVY?

Carol always kept up with campus activities. I was not surprised when one morning at breakfast she said she and a friend were going to the military department's open house, which was featuring a really big navy helicopter. The event offered tours of the helicopter, and Carol wanted to see it up close. I didn't learn about the results of the visit until I got home from work late that evening. Apparently, just as Carol and her friend were beginning to start their tour of the chopper, the pilot said, "We have to go to Fort Benning [now Fort Moore] and get fuel. Would you girls like to ride with us to Fort Benning?" I don't have to tell you Carol rapidly agreed and accepted the invitation for both her and her friend.

It was a totally routine flight to Fort Benning to secure fuel for the bird. But it provided an experience for Carol that she enjoyed relating to anyone who would listen.

CHAPTER 4

The Challenging Years

ACCOLADES FOR GALE

As a senior associate professor, I was hoping to become a full professor. I had long ago received tenure. It seemed everything was going my way. I learned that I was a candidate for full professor and that I had been awarded an alumni professorship. Hence my new title was to be alumni professor.

About this time, the college had received an endowment for support of sabbatical leaves for senior faculty. This sounded like a great idea. I had taken a short three-month sabbatical while I was an assistant professor. I had worked with a colleague in the Department of Biochemistry at the University of Georgia.

I decided to submit my application for a sabbatical to conduct research at the Weed Research Organization (WRO). WRO was a part of the federal research system of the United Kingdom and located in the city of Oxford, England. Soon after receiving the good news about the alumni professorship, I was awarded the Will Howard Smith Fellowship for sabbatical study in the UK.

This called for intense family planning. Of course, Carol encouraged me and assured me that she could handle the home front in my absence. Also, she, Judy, and Brad would visit me for two weeks during my sabbatical in the UK. They would try to come about midway during my stay.

During my first sabbatical at the University of Georgia in the Department of Biochemistry, I had stayed in the lab from eight in the morning until ten or eleven o'clock every night for the whole duration. I was bound and determined to enjoy this sabbatical a bit more, as well as see some of the country. In view of my plan, I advised my host for the sabbatical that I would work Monday, Tuesday, Wednesday, and Thursday. I would then reserve Friday, Saturday, and Sunday for holiday. Also, I bought both Brit Rail passes and Eurorail passes. These passes would enable me to ride the train anywhere in England or on the continent free of charge at any time in first class. All travel was covered except crossing the channel. This was only a few dollars via the hovercraft or an overnight steamer.

I arrived at the Weed Research Organization laboratory just before lunch one day. I quickly joined a group of scientists for lunch in the laboratory cafeteria. The menu for everybody was very simple. It consisted of bread, butter, cheese, and Guinness stout. I knew that I was going to enjoy my time in the UK.

For my sabbatical, I worked with my host on his research projects. We initiated experiments, collected data, analyzed data, and worked on summaries in preparation for publication. It was a great experience to see other ways of conducting experiments on issues that I was concerned with and interested in. I learned a great deal that I couldn't wait to implement when I got back home.

My first week was great, and I couldn't wait until Friday. I hadn't planned where to go, so I decided to take a simple train trip. I selected the city of Swansea, which is in the extreme western side of the UK on the coast. I selected it because it was only a simple train ride from Oxford to Swansea, with no required train changes. It simply started in Oxford and ended in Swansea.

I was greatly disappointed. Swansea was not a tourist town at all. In fact, it was only an overgrown fishing village. But anyway, I learned a great deal about navigating the train system and how to survive in another town, which would be helpful on my future trips.

After a week or so, I settled into a routine working Monday through Thursday and traveling Friday through Sunday.

Soon after I arrived at WRO, another weed scientist, Rolf Scoterud, from Norway, joined the laboratory. What's even more important is Rolf brought his automobile with him. But he was no better than me at driving on the "wrong" side of the road. As a result, we buddied up, and I was the designated assistant driver in helping him stay on the "correct" side of the road.

This was a great addition because it meant that we could take side trips during the early part of the week when we were both working. As a result, we made several trips to the Royal Shakespeare Theatre in Stratford-upon-Avon, only a couple hours from Oxford.

One especially noteworthy trip that I made was to the European Weed Science Conference scheduled in Marseille, France. Since the meeting was scheduled for a Monday, Tuesday, and Wednesday, I simply left the UK on Friday and ended up at the meeting site for the conference in Marseille on Sunday evening. The conference ended on Wednesday. This meant that I had four days for holiday and touring. Doing a map reconnaissance of the area, I selected several places in the south of France to visit. I really saw that area well.

I found that I ended up in Cannes, France, early on Saturday morning. I realized that the first order of business was to find a room for the evening. I learned there were absolutely no rooms available in the city of Cannes. The reason why? It was in the middle of the Cannes Film

Festival. So what was I to do? I truly enjoyed the day sight-seeing and gawking. There were film stars everywhere for the festival. There were a number of recognizable actors from the US as well as from other parts of the world.

One thing that caught my eye was a crowd of people that were down at the beach in front of one of the big hotels. Seeing the crowd of people, I had to go and see what the hullabaloo was all about. There was—I was told—a starlet, completely undressed with nothing on but a G-string frolicking around in the water. Obviously, there were dozens and dozens of photographers all trying to get the best shot. Of course, I couldn't pass up the opportunity, so I took my little thirty-five-millimeter camera and joined the photographers. Before I knew it, I was knee deep in water, but I had to get a great shot. I did get some great shots and had them developed as soon as I returned to Oxford. Unfortunately, I lost them before I got back to the US. Probably for the best.

Now it was getting later in the afternoon, and I did not have a place to sleep for the night. I knew that I had used up most of the day, and I was not able to stay up all night, so I had to find a place to sleep.

No problem. I headed to the train station and saw that there was a southbound train for Rome leaving in an hour or so. That sounded like the solution, so I caught the southbound train to Rome. I had dinner on the train. It took most of the night to get to Rome. I arrived in Rome about daylight.

After arriving in Rome, I went outside the train station to see what Rome looked like. I saw what I could see from the steps of the train station. I immediately went back inside and checked the train schedules. There was a northbound train leaving for Paris in a short time.

It would take all day to get from Rome back to Oxford by train. Believe it or not, I never saw any more of Rome than what I saw from the steps of the train station until I attended a UN FAO conference in Rome while I was undersecretary. I then saw Rome well.

Midway through my sabbatical, Carol, Judy, and Brad were scheduled to arrive. The plan was they were to fly directly from the US to

Frankfurt, Germany. To surprise Carol, I decided to grow a beard and mustache. When Carol and the kids saw me, they rolled with laughter! *Ouch!* Quietly, I shaved it all off that very night.

We would visit sites in Germany, then Switzerland, and go on to Paris. This took the first week. After Paris, we took the train to London. We crossed the channel in a hovercraft. After resting a bit on the weekend, we were off to Scotland on Monday. We took a night train from London to Inverness. I still remember what a pleasant trip it was. You couldn't help but sleep in that tremendous bed on the train, rocking back and forth. Truly one of the highlights of our trip. This trip included a cruise on Loch Ness. Brad fully expected to get a picture of the Loch Ness Monster. Unfortunately, the monster was asleep, and he didn't get a picture, but we did get a very enjoyable boat ride the length of Loch Ness.

Back in Oxford, we had one remaining night left. Rolf graciously agreed to take the whole family for one last visit to see a Shakespeare play in Stratford-upon-Avon. Another great experience. I am not sure I can remember the play, but it seemed like it was *As You Like It*.

All too soon it was time for Carol and the kids to say goodbye. I didn't want them to go.

I remained at the WRO for another three months before returning home with a multitude of new ideas for my research. Little did I know fate would intervene and I would never put into play many of the new ideas I had developed for my research program.

A NEW BEGINNING—SORT OF

Returning from my sabbatical in the UK, I was full of new ideas for my area of research, weed competition. I had gained new insight into some of the new techniques and ways of measuring the competitive relationship of weeds with crop plants. Consequently, I couldn't wait to get started on designing new experiments and planning for a busy season for research.

As soon as I returned from the UK, the first order of business was to see what my technicians and graduate students had accomplished while I was gone for several months. We were located at one of the branch stations about three hours from Auburn. We were visiting research plots that they had monitored while I was gone.

One of the station personnel brought me a message from the university vice president for agriculture. He wanted to visit with me. So I dropped everything and went to the office (this was before cell phones) and placed a call to the vice president's office. The vice president came right to the point. He wanted to see me. I responded that I would be visiting research plots and would be back in the office late Friday afternoon, so I could see him first thing Monday morning. He countered that he wanted to see me sooner than that, so I said, "Well, maybe we can wrap up with this location by the end of the day and I could see you on Friday." Exasperated, he said, "I want to see you now. Can you come now?" I got the picture and responded that I could leave my grad students and technician and borrow a vehicle from the station. I'd be in his office later that afternoon. He responded, "That's more like it."

Arriving in Auburn, I went straight to the vice president's office. I was still in obvious work clothes and boots. Hardly dressed appropriately to visit in the inner sanctum of the university. The vice president came straight to the point and said that he wanted me to be dean and director of the Alabama Agricultural Experiment Station.

I was in a quandary. I loved teaching and research, and I had many new ideas, having just returned from my sabbatical. I told him that in the past I had been contacted and urged to apply for administrative positions, but I didn't see where administrators made much difference, and they certainly didn't make much of a contribution. That was, perhaps, not quite the best thing to say to a senior administrator, but I said it anyway. The truth is, in fact, I didn't see how I could be as successful as an administrator as I had been as a teacher and researcher.

As with all my major decisions, I reserved the right to discuss the matter with Carol and told the vice president that I couldn't make a spur-of-the-moment decision. The vice president agreed. He suggested that I give him my answer the next morning.

That night, as I was talking with Carol, she saw the potential a bit better than I did and encouraged me to accept the challenge. To make matters even worse, I had recently been promoted to colonel (O-6) and had enrolled in Army War College at the Maxwell Air Force Base in Montgomery, Alabama. This was a very intense military training program that was important for someone to be considered for future promotion. Classes for the program met four hours four nights each week. This itself was a half-time job. Along with one full-time job as dean and director of the experiment station, it just wasn't feasible, so I reluctantly dropped the War College. This, of course, doomed any chances I might've had for promotion beyond colonel.

I realized I was burning the candle at both ends. The National Guard unit that I was assigned to was working closely with the Republic of Korea. As executive officer of the support group, I was sent to Korea frequently for a couple weeks each time. To make matters even worse, the university administration was in turmoil. While I was not immediately affected, my boss, the vice president for agriculture, was very much so. Soon, the university president was out, and there followed a couple of years of total uncertainty on the part of all administrators. During this difficult time for me, Carol seemed to find the unusual strength to provide just the right encouragement. Eventually, a new president was hired. That, unfortunately, presaged the beginning of the end for me at Auburn.

Such was my introduction into administration.

PROBLEMS FOR GALE

Little did I realize that 1985 would be a very challenging year for me—one that changed life, indeed, for our whole family. The new university president, Jim Martin, was a tough, take-no-prisoners type of administrator. My boss, Stan Wilson, also had a very strong personality and was a demanding administrator, but he had considerably more benevolent characteristics. Wilson had internal knowledge of the university and great clout throughout the state of Alabama, especially in the Alabama legislature. Obviously, these characteristics did not sit well with the new president, who wanted to be totally in charge. Soon they clashed, and my boss was terminated. Since he did not have tenure, he was simply dismissed from the university. This development left me as the senior administrator left standing in agriculture.

The new president, having eliminated his competition, then proceeded to consolidate his power base. He did this by planning a complete restructuring of the university, particularly the agricultural programs. The result of his proposed plan would ensure that agricultural interest and personnel would not offer any competition. The proposed plan would obviously result in considerable loss of recognition for agriculture and less influence around the state. Consequently, as the senior administrator remaining in agriculture, I had no choice but to offer resistance to his plan.

Initially, my effort was to try to use a logical approach by seeking dialogue and even compromise such that we both could accept. Since the university president held all the aces, this was not in the cards. Eventually, after several months, the die was cast: no compromise, no change to the president's plan. The president won all the points of the controversy. I was left to try other tactics. When you're lacking power, you must seek it from other sources. I was able to mobilize help from some of my senior tenured faculty, leadership of several powerful commodity groups throughout the state, some of the senior agricultural administrators of neighboring states including Louisiana, Georgia, and Mississippi, and especially from key members of the Alabama legislative body.

The clinching action of this effort was a hearing in the state capital by a joint House–Senate committee favorable to my position.

What a show! Support for my position was provided by a few senior, tenured faculty, select neighboring experiment directors, and several representatives of major commodity groups, while the university administration was represented by the university president and staff and the chairman of the university faculty senate. The committee hearing went well. As a result, we now had plans to hold the university budget hostage until the president agreed to our position on the structure of agriculture. Consequently, at the end of the hearing, we thought we had won.

Late that evening, I got a call from one of the key supporters of our position. Apparently, more powerful legislators had said that there would be no way the legislature would hold the university budget hostage for agriculture. So a win quickly turned into a loss. I knew immediately that I was toast. The president, of course, had no recourse but to terminate my role as dean and director of the Alabama Agricultural Experiment Station.

Since I was a tenured professor, the president could not terminate my faculty appointment without revoking my tenure. In a university, the president does not have the power to revoke tenure (unless an exigency is declared) until it's recommended by the faculty tenure committee, and I knew that I had not done anything that would violate protocols for revoking tenure.

Consequently, the president had no choice but to allow me to return to the faculty position I had held before joining the administration.

All of this is to say, these were some of the lowest points of my young administrative career. Being terminated (fired) from what I now considered my dream job hurt deeply. But at this exceedingly low point, Carol seemed to rise to an unexpected level. She didn't wallow in self-pity—nor would she allow me to feel sorry for myself. Quite the opposite: she became a fighter. She challenged me to not lose faith and not to become bitter. She also would not allow me to use the term *fired*. We finally settled on using the term *terminated*. I always thought that was kind of funny.

I will forever be indebted to Carol for how she handled my termination. She focused on the better days ahead. My advice to anyone who plans to be fired is to have a wife such as Carol who won't let you feel sorry for yourself or let you give up.

I soon adapted to a new reality. In my last days as a director, and still in control of the experiment station budget, I set myself up for research. I didn't waste any money, but I did get myself set up to ensure I would have all I needed to conduct a successful research program. I had been a successful teacher/researcher in the past, and I was totally confident I could do it again, especially with Carol's help.

STARTING OVER

The events surrounding the new university president and his actions leading to my termination as dean and director of the Alabama Agricultural Experiment Station were shattering to me. Carol was my rock during all this turmoil. There was only one time I had to come to Carol's aid.

Carol and I were attending an event at Brad's school, and we happened to run into the university senior vice president's wife. She proceeded to make comments to Carol about me and my termination. There were things said that Carol deemed inappropriate. Carol began to respond in a quite forceful manner. As quickly as I could, I got us separated and out of contact. I won't say any more.

But we survived, thanks to Carol. She convinced me I had lost a major battle but I had not lost the war. So I did what I had always done—threw myself into making plans to restart my teaching and research program. Remember, I was full of new ideas for my research after returning from sabbatical some five years earlier.

As the end of the year approached, I saw an announcement about an open position for an associate director/resident director in Tifton, Georgia. I realized I had put Carol through a lot during my aborted administrative career in the past five years. While reluctant at first, I had grown to enjoy being an administrator. I was hesitant to even mention it to her, but I did. Of course, her response was quite positive. It seemed like a challenge, so she told me to go for it. It seemed Carol had more confidence in me than I had in myself. I had already made my mind up to stay at Auburn University, just finishing my career as a teacher/researcher. But her encouragement gave me a new lease on life. I would not disappoint her or me. So I applied.

Competition for the position was quite formidable. Candidates included a USDA senior scientist and a couple of internal candidates, as well as a recently fired former director from Auburn. Betting odds were that I would not even show, let alone win. But I did win the job and truly began a new professional life.

On the first day of the job, one of the internal candidates came by the office to congratulate me as well as to inform me that it was not every day that "the second-best candidate for a senior position gets the job." The losing candidate, Dale Threadgill, later turned out to be one of my best department heads after I became dean, but that's another story.

I was to start to work in April. That meant Carol would stay in Auburn with the children, sell the house, work with the movers, and take care of all the details. All I had to do was go to Tifton and begin my new job. Carol handled all the details in a very fine fashion. After selling the house in Auburn, Carol and Brad joined me in Tifton, and immediately I asked her to find us a new house. The apartment we were living in was quite small. Judy was in school at Auburn and continued to live in the dorm.

CHAPTER 5

Our Sojourn in South Georgia

ADAPTING TO SOUTH GEORGIA

Until I accepted the job as resident director of the Coastal Plain Experiment Station, we had lived only in Auburn while I worked for Auburn University. Since we were both totally Southern, it was a bit hard to realize the differences among regions within the South. The atmosphere and pace of life in deep South Georgia was quite different from what we had experienced in Auburn or in our earlier lives in Mobile, Alabama, Gainesville, Florida, Ames, Iowa, Opelika, Alabama, or Bastrop, Louisiana. But we adapted—although a bit slowly.

Carol had identified and we had negotiated for the purchase of about twenty-five acres of land that included three lakes. The acreage was sufficient such that we were able to have a large garden and even get a few cows. While I was never successful in turning Carol into a farm girl, she did show a great interest in my small herd of White Park cattle.

The White Park breed was developed during the Middle Ages in England to forage grass around the castles and moats of the day. As a result, the breed apparently evolved into very docile cattle. In fact, one could say they were just nothing but huge, grass-consuming pets.

Almost as soon as the cattle arrived, Carol seemed to think each animal should have a name. Of course, she could not remember their names the next day. There was one exception. After I bought a White Park herd bull and she heard him bellow a couple of times, she pointed out that he was a tenor. Consequently, from then on my herd bull was Pavarotti.

Two White Park calves from our first breeding year.

The house was situated directly on one of the smaller lakes. Because the house was a bit isolated, Carol soon sought a more challenging venue. She got a part-time job at Abraham Baldwin Agricultural College (ABAC), which is adjacent to the Coastal Plain Experiment Station, where I worked. This job provided an opportunity for her to take some courses at ABAC.

During these early years in Tifton, Carol tried to become more involved. She joined the choir in our local church, but we did not make many friends. As a station director, I didn't think it appropriate to socialize with my colleagues at work, and we were completely new in town. Eventually, old depression made its way back into Carol's life. It didn't help that Brad had opted for the army directly out of high school rather than go to college.

At home on the lake and acreage, things were a bit problematic. We soon learned that our homesite on the lake was quite a pleasant building site, but not perfect. Just as we enjoyed the location close to water, cottonmouth moccasins also considered it a very livable habitat. One afternoon Carol was strolling in the backyard by one of the small lakes and almost stepped on a five-foot cottonmouth. Frightened, she wheeled and, in the process, broke her ankle. After getting Carol in the house quickly, I was able to dispatch this cottonmouth to snake heaven with a blast of my twelve-gauge shotgun.

The experience with the cottonmouth caused us both to be concerned about our location. Carol used the pasture by the lake for her walking routine. To prevent Carol from getting surprised by another cottonmouth, I mowed a clear path completely around our pasture by the large lake so that it would be easy to spot any future snakes across her path. I kept the path mowed for the remaining days of the summer.

EVIDENCE OF A MOTHER'S LOVE

Nothing, absolutely nothing, brings out a mother's love for her children as do conflicting emotions such as joy and fear. Carol experienced and dealt with both concurrently.

Several events and changes began occurring that would affect our family. I had accepted a new job in Tifton, Georgia. We were leaving Auburn, where we had lived for over twenty years. Judy graduated from Auburn University and was planning a late summer wedding.

The wedding date was set well in advance so there was ample time for planning, which was certainly needed in view of several complications. Judy had relocated to Birmingham, Alabama, for employment. Her fiancé, Sammy, and his family lived in Birmingham, as did many of her college friends. Since the details of the wedding are the bride's decision, Judy chose a wedding in Birmingham.

Needless to say, this was a very electrifying time for Carol. She was deeply involved in all aspects of planning the wedding. She was in constant contact with Judy and the future in-laws. As the father of the bride, I barely made the level of an afterthought. My only role in the big event was to sign my name a few times…on checks. For several months, our household was consumed by the wedding decisions. Carol was giddy with happiness for Judy.

Months before the wedding date, the "temperature" in the Middle East was rising. This instability eventually led to Iraq invading Kuwait. US President George H. W. Bush made it abundantly clear this invasion by Iraq of a sovereign country would not stand. It was about this time that I had completed my term as commandant of the Alabama Military Academy and was quickly assigned to a military unit that was expected to also be deployed to Iraq in the Middle East.

I don't know why, but as always, when times were tough, Carol seemed to get renewed strength. For a few months we assumed that both Brad and I would be in Iraq. In the final analysis, mobilization of my unit was scrubbed, and we were not deployed. As a result, I did not join Brad in the Gulf War.

The situation escalated to a climax only weeks before the wedding date. At the time, Brad was assigned to the Twenty-Fourth Mechanized Infantry Division at Fort Stewart, Georgia, near Savannah. President Bush soon announced Operation Desert Shield to protect Kuwait. The first major unit targeted for deployment to implement Desert Shield was the Twenty-Fourth Division, Brad's unit.

The announcement of a unit's deployment results in an unbelievable cascade of events—especially when there are anticipated hostilities. Brad volunteered for the advanced party to accompany the ship used to transport his unit's combat equipment. They shipped out of the port of Savannah only days before Judy's wedding.

These actions threw a curveball at the wedding plans. Brad was a part of the wedding party and had certain responsibilities. Quickly, plans were made for someone else to cover Brad's responsibilities, thus enabling the wedding plans to progress smoothly.

Now Carol had to balance her happiness for Judy on this, her special day, with anxiety and stark terror about Brad on a ship in the mid-Atlantic heading for war. While I had a minute role in the wedding, I was an equal partner in concern for Brad. Very soon, Desert Shield morphed into Desert Storm, which initiated the start of the Gulf War. Indeed, it was exceedingly impressive to watch Carol living through these very difficult days while our son was at war. She kept up with Brad and his unit in the daily newspaper. She always kept a positive attitude and knew that Brad would survive. As a result, I had to include in this book a poem written by Brad, "To My Mother When Gone to War."

Of course, we all knew what Brad's response to the situation would be. He would simply say, "Don't worry. Just suck it up!" Well, we did not just suck it up, but we did get Judy married in a fine fashion and off to her honeymoon.

After saying goodbyes to the newly married couple, wedding guests, and our new in-law's family, Carol and I hosted her entire family for an evening meal at Lloyd's, one of Birmingham's great family restaurants.

As we looked back at these two memorable events, Carol and I were thankful for the gracious blessings bestowed upon us and our children: Judy's marriage ceremony and Brad enduring the fairly short but intense war unharmed and returning home safely. Carol happily continued to be an affectionate, loving wife and mother.

The safe return of our son to Fort Stewart upon the unit's return was truly one of the highlights of our life. Our son was a combat veteran. While I had been in the army almost thirty years, I had never experienced a combat deployment. We were exceedingly proud of our son.

This latter event provided an opportunity for a beautiful example of Carol's motherly love for her son. In fact, I didn't learn about this until Carol's funeral. While Carol and I had few secrets from each other, I learned of this after her death! I'm sure Carol kept this from me because she knew I would not approve. I suspect she knew it would be a confrontation from which she would not back down, and neither would I. Carol had told Brad she would help him escape to Canada to avoid going to war. But Brad made his own decision. That decision is so elegantly expressed in Brad's poem to his mother in this book.

As a husband and father, I can say that the actions of both Carol and Brad over this issue are some of the proudest moments of my life.

As an afterthought, I noted that after my unit was alerted for possible mobilization and deployment, Carol did not offer me any help for escape to Canada!

Carol did not have to carry these heavy emotions on her own. I was there for her when she needed to express her feelings, which were often frustration and fear in relation to Brad's deployment. I also was prepared to listen to her concerns about Judy and the wedding. That is what husbands and wives do, and that's what we did throughout our marriage.

OLD DEMON DEPRESSION RETURNS

It is not surprising that during periods of my traveling Carol carried such a heavy load. This eventually ended with another bout of depression. She now better understood her problem and took many steps to help herself. After getting a part-time job at ABAC, she enrolled in the school and registered for some classes. She was seeing a doctor on a regular basis and was receiving a new antidepressant about as soon as a new one was released.

Since the house was a bit isolated, I don't think that helped much. She decided she would be better off living in town. So she rented an apartment in Tifton. As director of the station, I never discussed my personal life with anyone. Eventually, it became known that Carol had rented an apartment in town, so the obvious conclusion was that we were having marital problems and were separating. I didn't help by just smiling when someone tried to seek personal information about my life. It really was a bit unusual, but as an administrator I always felt my personal life was mine and the less said about me, the better.

Almost as soon as the episode of depression manifested itself, it dissipated. When I thought I learned something about depression, the more I realized I didn't know anything. My only conclusion is, I feel very deeply for individuals who suffer from this debilitating disease.

As things were settling down, Carol saw an ad in the Atlanta paper that Pavarotti was going to give a concert at the Fox Theatre in Atlanta. Carol was beside herself.

A KISS FROM PAVAROTTI

Hearing the news about Pavarotti's coming to the Fox in Atlanta didn't particularly float my boat. But I could see Carol was serious, so I encouraged her to plan to go. She started planning. This was such a great event for her. She wanted to share it with some of her siblings. Consequently, she called, and a couple of her siblings agreed to drive up from Mobile. She would get tickets and take them to the Fox Theatre in Atlanta to see (hear) Pavarotti.

Carol's picture of Pavarotti. Not sure what the
words say, but apparently Carol treasured his photo.

While Atlanta was only four hours away, her siblings had to drive all
the way from Mobile—five or six hours to our house. Carol handled
all the details of her entourage, and they headed to Atlanta.

Apparently, Pavarotti gave his usual outstanding performance, but
do you think that was enough for Carol? Of course not. She led her
brother and sister backstage until they were able to get to Pavarotti's
dressing room. They proceeded to dialogue with Pavarotti. Lo and behold, as they were saying their goodbyes, Pavarotti gave Carol a great
big kiss. She remembered that kiss as long as she lived, and so did I.

BECOMING A VALDOSTA CITIZEN

Our house in Tifton was five miles south of the city, so the commute to Valdosta was less than twenty minutes via I-75. This seemed like a quite workable commute. I knew her courses and work in the department were going well, so I was shocked when one night at dinner she abruptly said she had found a house adjacent to the Valdosta State College (VSC) campus she wanted to buy. Knowing Carol, I surmised that she had already negotiated to buy the house, maybe even had bought it, but certainly wanted to run it by me before proceeding. I never knew if that was a fact or not. Anyway, she explained that this would greatly facilitate her work in the department as well as her coursework. How could I not be supportive?

For the next several months, I lived in the house on the lake with the snakes, and Carol lived adjacent to the VSC campus in the great city of Valdosta. While this sounds like a drastic change, it really facilitated both her work and mine. I spent each weekend, Friday through Monday, with Carol in Valdosta and enjoyed the ambience of living in the city. I'm not sure what others might have thought about our arrangement, but we both seemed to think it a great solution for our situation. Carol would come to Tifton when there was an event or activity that required my spouse. This was a very workable arrangement until there was a family crisis. Her uncle Earl, who lived in Montgomery, became very ill, and since he and her aunt Judy had no children, it was up to Carol to provide family support. This became exceedingly demanding. This unexpected commitment eventually caused Carol to have to drop out of school, losing her scholarship as well as her job in the English department.

As usual Carol did what had to be done to support those she loved, even though it cost her dearly.

Even after the death of her uncle, she never put things back together again at VSC. She did keep the house for a couple more years. Frankly, it was a bit exciting for me to live in Tifton and then leave Tifton on Friday and visit Carol and the cats for a long weekend each week.

Eventually, Carol decided to sell it even though I thought it was a good investment.

GALE GETS A BEAGLE

While living by the lake, we had discussed the possibility of getting a dog. Growing up, I had the responsibility of feeding and caring for my father's pack of foxhounds. This was not always a pleasant task. Besides, they were not my dogs and hardly the kind of dogs a young boy would like anyway. Consequently, growing up, I never had a dog of my own. So Carol asked Judy to find a beagle pup for my birthday. This was a complete surprise to me.

A beagle was not a new idea. My children had brought their two beagles from Auburn when we relocated to Tifton. But they were not my dogs. Besides, they were getting old, and Carol knew that I liked beagles. When Judy visited for my birthday, she brought Carol's birthday present for me. I immediately fell in love with my very own dog, and I named her Happy.

I was quite pleased with Happy. Eventually, Happy had a litter of her own. I think my neighbor's Rottweiler was the father. I kept one of the pups. He was such a strong dog, even as a puppy, that I named him Patton, of course after the general. Before Patton was full grown, his mother, Happy, met an untimely death. While I never had any proof, I'm quite convinced that her previous lover—the Rottie—killed her. So sad!

Patton thrived. He had many of the traits of Happy but was far more aggressive. One of his favorite pastimes was barking and trying to frighten small alligators that were frequently exiting the lake. This continued for some time. Again, I have no proof; however, I surmised that Patton started playing and barking at larger gators. He failed to appreciate how quickly a gator can lunge and unfortunately served as a delicious meal for some unknown gator.

Our house by the lakes in Tifton was a great experience. We enjoyed the lakes, always mindful of the cottonmouths and gators. There were plenty of fish for both us and the gators. In fact, Carol caught a huge, speckled perch—not a record, but very close to it. Just to be clear, I never caught one even close to the size of Carol's "Old Gus." In the tightknit research community, it was soon common knowledge that the director's wife had landed a near record speckled perch in their lake. My department head of entomology, Dr. Max Bass, wrote a poem commemorating Carol's fishing success. Of course, I had Carol's Old Gus mounted.

After reading "Ode to a Special Speckled Perch," I encouraged Dr. Bass to stick to entomology!

"Old Gus," caught by Carol in our large lake in 1994.

(Note: The weight of Gus the Great was estimated by a reliable source as perhaps somewhat under eight pounds. He was caught by Carol Buchanan during the spring of 1994 using a cane pole.)

Ode to a Special Speckled Perch

by Max H. Bass for Carol Buchanan

To the pond I strode,
    Cane pole in hand;
Fire in my belly,
    Worms in a can.
I knew that ole Gus
    Lay deep in the water;
I knew that today
    To catch him I oughter.
I baited my hook,
    Cast in with great joy;
The water did swirl,
    I had found the ole boy!
The float went under,
    Fate was at hand;
I clutched my pole,
    I took my stand.
The pole bent,
    The line did stretch;
With all my strength,
    I held that wretch.
I pulled, he pulled;
    It went on and on.
And then with a shudder,
    His fight was gone.
With a mighty pull,
    I put Gus on the ground,
And listened closely
    For trumpets to sound.
And there for all wondering
    Eyes to behold
Was Gus the goliath,
    Of fame untold.

(This slick, slithery, slimy, speckled, finny, fishy denizen of the deep; this mighty, monstrous monarch of the mud; this epic example of evolutionary excellence; this famous, furious, fighting fish; this Gus.)

CLASSICAL GUITAR

Carol was born into a musical family. Both her father and mother as well as siblings inherited interest in music along with musical talent. Her father was a professional, as well as her brother. Of course, my musical talent ended with getting a song on the radio.

I was not surprised when Carol wanted to learn to play the classical guitar. So we bought a guitar. After paying $1,000 for one guitar, I thought it should play itself. But she signed up for lessons and practiced constantly. While I didn't play, I loved to hear classical guitar music even when she was practicing. So I was not totally surprised early one Saturday morning as we were having breakfast when she said casually there was a great event in Tampa that featured some of the world's top classical guitar players. The show was scheduled for that evening. She casually stated that this would be a great opportunity to hear three of the world's greatest classical guitar players. She then followed that if we got dressed quickly, we could get there in plenty of time to have dinner and attend the concert. So within the hour we were dressed and in the car on I-75 southbound for Tampa, Florida— only 230 miles away.

We found a nice hotel, and the concierge was quite helpful with getting tickets to the concert as well as recommending a great seafood restaurant that was very close by. Things were going quite well.

What a great concert! We got back to the hotel around midnight and slept late the next morning. We finally arrived home late Sunday evening. What a great experience!

ELARIO

The following event unfolded quite naturally. New Orleans was always our second favorite city in the US. Of course, San Francisco was number one because that was where we really started our marriage, but New Orleans was always a very close second. Carol and her family had lived in New Orleans while her father went to seminary. I was scheduled to attend a conference in New Orleans, and Carol decided to accompany me. We got reservations at one of the hotels in the French Quarter. We both noted that the lounge featured an entertainer named Elario. I've always been skeptical of people who have only one name, but it sounded like a good show. All the advertisements for the Elario show seemed impressive. So we had dinner, then headed for the early show. It was a great show. During the intermission, Carol just had to visit Elario. So she led the way, and after a few questions and talking to the right people, we got to Elario. After a little while, you would've thought that Carol and Elario were old friends. So we stayed for the second show as well. After the show, we said goodbye to Elario, and Carol assured him we would be back before his contract with the hotel was up.

You guessed it! We did make it back—in fact, three times over the next few months—one time for another meeting, and two more times by just driving over from Mobile.

Now that Carol is gone, I must find a home for all of Elario's records.

CHAPTER 6

The Athens Years

AN UNEXPECTED RELOCATION

After eight or nine years, Carol and I had adapted to life in South Georgia. While Carol still experienced some depression, she was being more effective in dealing with it. I was thriving as an administrator. Putting the sour taste of Auburn behind me, I felt I was making reasonable and significant progress in leading a major agricultural research program. After the tumultuous years at Auburn, I felt I had grown as an administrator. I was totally comfortable in making the myriad decisions required of an administrator. It was even more pleasing to realize that I had total support from all levels of upper administration, including the university president. It was pretty close to a perfect job. I had full authority over my campus. I only saw my supervising boss maybe four or five times a year. What more could one ask for?

We had survived the snakes and gators and getting our son back from the war, and now he was enrolled at the University of Georgia. There was no good reason to want to leave South Georgia at this time.

Our idyllic life was about to end. My supervisor, Clive Donoho, who was very special to me because he had hired me even though I had been terminated, decided to retire. Upon receiving this news, the dean asked me if I would agree to serve as interim director of the Georgia Agricultural Experiment Station system. Since I was the senior associate director of the system, I had little choice but to accept his offer. Assuming this to be a temporary assignment, I negotiated with the dean to do the interim director job in travel status. This would allow me to be in Athens Monday through Friday and return to Tifton Friday afternoon until Monday morning. It still would not cause us to alter our new life plan to remain in Tifton until our planned final retirement.

In view of these developments, I was not surprised when late one Friday afternoon Carol met me with an urgent opportunity. She was bubbling with excitement. She related she had found our perfect retirement home just south of Tifton, in Adel, Georgia. Carol had found this one-hundred-plus-year-old house that had in earlier years been the local hospital. It had been completely renovated and converted into the mayor's residence, with all the modern amenities.

After completing the purchase, we had to relocate, among a myriad of other chores and responsibilities. I had a local moving company move the heavy things, while I was going to handle all the light things by myself in my truck.

No sooner had we completed this relocation and moved into our new home in Adel than another bombshell dropped at work. The dean announced his pending retirement.

Carol and I had long discussions regarding this development while we were thinking about retirement. I still had to work at least five or six more years before I could retire. I wasn't particularly looking forward to a new job. However, sometimes you have to think strategically. A new dean or director could make my great job in Tifton a much less desirable job for my last years. On the other hand, if I were the new dean, I would have more control of our future. Such thoughts were controlling our discussion about our future. As usual Carol urged me to go for it, but at the same time she would be very happy staying in Adel while I finished my career.

As a result of these discussions, we decided that probably our best hope for a more peaceful completion of our career would be for me to at least make an effort and become a candidate for the new position of dean of the College of Agricultural and Environmental Sciences.

Carol seemed to enjoy the interview process. I was pleased that a friend had been assigned by the dean to serve as our liaison for this process.

After extensive interviews, the president made his decision. My appointment was to be announced in Athens for all local faculty and staff and other personnel in each of the counties in Georgia as well as the branch stations, and both the Tifton and Griffin campuses were to be announced electronically via satellite. Of course, this was before Zoom became available.

Carol related later she was a bit frightened when President Knapp, who was moderating my acceptance presentation, said, "Gale, you now have full authority and responsibility for everything the College of Agriculture does and does not do. Good luck." With that he left the stage and turned the college over to me.

I was the new dean and director of the College of Agricultural and Environmental Sciences at the University of Georgia.

BECOMING AN ATHENS RESIDENT

After we had decided that I should become a candidate for dean and director, we never looked back. I was a bit apprehensive knowing the quality of all candidates. Carol, from the beginning, just assumed I would be appointed dean and director and that we would relocate to Athens.

We had hardly gotten established in our new (old) house in Adel. So what would we do for housing in Athens? Selling our home in Adel was out of the question, for it was Carol's dream home. We both agreed that an apartment was probably best for our sojourn in Athens.

Searching for an apartment in Athens, a major college town, was indeed challenging. I recalled my experience when my brother, Randall, and I were searching for an apartment at the University of Florida. The year I started graduate school, he was a freshman, and we searched all day, never finding an acceptable apartment. On the way home, we saw a billboard that offered "Buy your own new home for $9,999.99." We felt that had some potential, so we turned around and headed back to the address on the billboard. Within an hour I had bought a house that was to be completed within the next week or so.

Anyway, Carol and I started looking for an apartment in Athens. In the first three apartments we visited, there was a great presence of comely co-eds. Carol saw that so many young women would not be in the best interest for us, so we kept looking. On the second day, we found what we were looking for.

We found an apartment complex a little farther out of town that catered to a much older clientele. It just seemed to fit our expectations. As it turned out, the apartment was such a great fit for us that we lived in it for the whole time I served as dean—almost ten years.

ADAPTING TO LIFE AS A DEAN'S WIFE

The first few months in Athens were almost a blur. We had brought only limited items from Adel for our apartment. Carol really enjoyed shopping and finding just what she thought we needed to live comfortably. She quickly converted the second bedroom in the apartment into her computer room.

For the first few years, she enjoyed the many occasions when I was involved in and expected to attend a function with my spouse. One of the events she enjoyed the most was the extension's annual conference. One activity at the conference was the auction for support of the state 4-H program. I found several items for which Carol had been the successful bidder when cleaning out the house after her death. One item I'm still trying to figure out. Why did she bid on and win the fender of NASCAR driver Kevin Harvick's wrecked car? It's authentic and has the papers to say that it did come from Kevin Harvick's wrecked car. Since it's authentic, would you like to buy it?

Carol enjoyed exploring Athens. She found places I had never heard about. Old, off the beaten path bookstores were here favorite. She could also sniff out novelty stores that sold just about everything, or as I told her—junk. But she always enjoyed such excursions.

Football games were always a very special and exciting day. Since the college often had guests for the game, it was really a workday for the dean and his wife. This always included many events, receptions, and sitting with guests in the university president's box for the game.

While we didn't socialize individually with faculty and staff in the college, we always hosted a Christmas reception for all faculty and administrators. Our first such event was held in the common facilities area at the headquarters of the apartment complex. While this was quite satisfactory, we found an even better place to host our Christmas reception—the State Botanical Garden of Georgia at the University of Georgia.

THE SECOND VISIT TO HAWAII

Since our honeymoon at the first International Weed Science Conference in Davis, California, Carol had not been keen on attending scientific or professional meetings. However, I was active in some organizations such as Farm Foundation that encouraged spouse attendance.

As soon as I learned that the winter meetings of Farm Foundation were scheduled for January in Hawaii, I mentioned to Carol the possibility of her accompanying me. The first response was, "Been there, done that." I explained this was a completely different kind of meeting than the first time we went to Hawaii. First, the Farm Foundation is composed of people from many parts of the country and represents a highly diverse range of professions. This included farmers with very large farms, important business executives, and government leaders who represent many different types of organizations and institutions. There would also be only a very few academic types like me. The diversity of participants stimulated her interest. I further explained we would be visiting the Big Island and totally focused on agriculture and agriculturally related topics. Shopping was not a priority item or even on the agenda.

This turned out to be one of the most enjoyable trips we ever made as husband and wife. Farm Foundation had selected a beautiful hotel between the ocean on the west and the volcano on the east on the Big Island. We had a beachside room on the second floor, so we could leave the sliding doors open and hear the waves as we drifted off to sleep each night. An added attraction was watching whales swim yards off the beach. This was truly a great experience.

The tours were designed to appeal both to members and their spouses. Of course, Hawaiian agriculture is quite impressive. One very interesting visit was to the Parker Ranch, one of the largest cattle ranches in the US. We both really enjoyed seeing this huge cattle ranch up close.

While the technical sessions were open to all spouses, if they desired, they could enjoy the beach, watch whales, or sleep in.

In fact, Carol had such a great time she opted to stay a few days after the completion of the Farm Foundation meeting and participate in some additional tours. She had the opportunity to meet and visit with one of my best friends, Hub Daniel, and his wife, Pat, on some of the excursions. Unfortunately, I had to return to Georgia for pressing meetings and activities. The second Hawaiian visit was a great experience—much more enjoyable than our first.

THE BUSH INAUGURATION

For a number of years, Bob Redding of the Washington, DC–based Redding Firm had helped me with my Washington congressional contacts regarding special grants. In fact, he had previously worked with me during my days as resident director in Tifton and all the years I worked as dean and director. He mentioned one day the possibility of attending the inauguration of President George W. Bush. Both Carol and I were intrigued by the possibility of attending an inauguration.

Gale and Carol in front of the US Capitol on the inauguration day for President George W. Bush. At this time, I did not know that I would be joining his administration.

We started early enough to enable us to get a hotel room in the downtown area that was very close to the Capitol. Bob was hosting a big dinner for all the clients of his consulting firm.

Carol and I had many questions. We had never been to a presidential inauguration before. But we did what thousands of others did. We just followed our instincts, and that worked out very well. Bob got us tickets to some of the events—especially those that had relations to agriculture.

What an experience! First, on Inauguration Day we rose about 4:00 a.m. and dressed quickly so we could get into the grounds and as close to the front of the inauguration stand as possible. Of course, the best sites in front of the inauguration stands were standing-only sites. You had to be a US senator or top donor to get close enough to get a chair. We did not fit either category. But we were lucky. We did get inside the grounds closest to the inauguration stands. We got to our standing position about 6:00 a.m. The program was scheduled to start at twelve o'clock. That means we stood in one place for over seven hours to attend the inauguration.

It's hard to believe we stood in place for that long. Of all times to forget my camera, I had forgotten it. However, a nice couple from Ohio graciously agreed to take a picture of us and then send it to us in the mail. Believe it or not, a few days after returning home, we got a nice note from the couple and a picture.

CAROL'S IRELAND ADVENTURE

While living in Auburn, we became good friends with the Glydes. Professor Glyde was a distinguished professor of music and well known in music circles throughout the country. His wife, Dorothy, was a delightful person. They were both very active in the local humane society in Auburn. Carol and our children were also very active in the Humane Society and developed a close friendship with the Glyde family.

No surprise, the Glydes were close friends even though I was in agriculture and even associated with those "nasty" chemicals called herbicides. But we remained close friends. We were all saddened by the death of Professor Glyde. After his death Carol made a point to maintain a close relationship with Mrs. Glyde. This relationship persisted long after we left Auburn.

It was not a surprise when one night at dinner, Carol stated to no one in particular, wouldn't it be interesting if she and Mrs. Glyde took a trip. Knowing Carol, I surmised that she had already planned this interesting trip that she had just thought about. This was several years after the death of Professor Glyde, and Mrs. Glyde was living with one of her children in different locations around the US. My response to her rhetorical question was that "this sounds like a great idea." Of course, my next question was, "Where do you plan to go?" Since the recent rhetorical question, I thought we were in the early stages of this idea for a trip. However, Carol quickly responded quite knowledgeably—Ireland. Why Ireland? At the time, I had no idea, although later I learned the family of Carol's father was from Ireland. Carol's father had a beautiful Irish tenor voice. These facts might have sparked Carol's interest in a trip to Ireland. I truly wish I knew what prompted the choice for a girls' trip. I use the term *girls* even though by this time Carol was youthfully middle aged and Mrs. Glyde was—let's just say—active, spry, and quite elderly.

Now that Carol had my endorsement—she knew she didn't really need it—she started making plans for both her and Mrs. Glyde. First, get passports. Hers was up to date, but she had to start at the beginning with Mrs. Glyde.

By now Carol was an old hand at international travel. She soon had airfare, hotels for the first couple of days, and car rental. What? I questioned her about the car rental. She responded quickly that they wanted to see the country, and the only way to really see it was if they had their own transportation and could go where they wished. I reminded her of our experience in the UK many years earlier and how difficult it was to drive on the "wrong" side of the road. She gave me that "mind your own business, I can handle it" look, and that ended the conversation.

For this trip there were no second thoughts of changing plans. While I can relate only a few things about the trip—those that Carol wished to share—they must have had a great time, a real ball.

Upon their return, my first question was, "Did you really drive all over Ireland?" Carol responded, "Of course we did, and there were no problems."

Their plan was to land in Dublin and spend a couple of days seeing the capital city before beginning to travel around the countryside. Soon after arriving in Dublin, they encountered an advertisement for a hit play just in from America. The hotel had displays, and everyone was talking about the new American play. Even the hotel staff told them about the play and how to get tickets. Of course, this just whetted the girls' artsy appetites. They had to get tickets and see it because it was new from America. They got tickets for the first night. They dressed in their best outfits and headed for the theater to see the play *Angels in America*. No further comment needs to be made.

As it turns out, the remainder of the Ireland trip was fantastic. One of the real highlights occurred quite serendipitously. They were checking in at a hotel in Sligo after a full day of sight-seeing. The hotel personnel questioned if they were checking in for the usual party for the celebration of Yeats's birthday. I might add Yeats was always one of Carol's favorite poets. They explained they were not aware, and they were just tourists and wanted to spend the night in this beautiful city they had heard so much about. Carol quickly added that Yeats was her favorite poet and wished they had tickets. No problem, the hotel clerk said she could arrange for them to get tickets. As a result, quite unexpectedly and unplanned, Carol and Dorothy attended the annual celebration of Yeats's birthday in his hometown. This had to be the highlight of their Ireland trip.

Apparently, Carol and Dorothy had a very enjoyable trip and got to see Ireland up close. Fortunately, in later years I got to see Ireland when I was invited to speak at a celebration of the founding of the agricultural research system for Ireland. My sight-seeing was limited to visits to several research stations and laboratories.

The Glydes remained some of our closest friends. In later years, I'm still reminded of the Glydes every time I go into my work room. Upon Professor Glyde's death, Dorothy insisted that I take all of his yard tools and shop equipment, including spare nails, screws, bolts, and all of his "stuff." I still have much of what I inherited.

The last time we saw Dorothy was while we were living in Washington. We decided to take a train trip up to Connecticut where she was living with one of her daughters. We spent several wonderful days with her in Connecticut. This was just a very short time before her death. At the train station, we rented a car. The only one they had available was a big red Cadillac, which they let us have at a good price. So we took it. A highlight of the visit was touring as much of Connecticut as you can see in a full day. I served as chauffeur for the two girls, who sat in the back seat and talked for a whole day. Dorothy treated us to a Connecticut lunch.

CAROL GETS A CADILLAC

Soon after getting settled in Athens, we realized our car—a vintage Chrysler—was not what it used to be. If we were going to make frequent trips back to Adel, we thought we needed a new car. She explained we would be driving from Athens to the farm and to see her folks in Mobile, so we just needed a better car. I told her I was just too busy to worry about trying to search for a new car. Maybe she could do the car shopping. I further suggested, "Why don't you ask Brad to help you with your car shopping?" Obviously, I had not given this proper thought, because a few years earlier when Brad had needed a vehicle, I had turned Carol and Brad loose to buy a respectable student vehicle for him. I was fully expecting a small used car with good tires. They ended up buying about the opposite of what he really needed. They came home with a Jeep, ready for travel in the Outback.

With my suggestions, I anticipated I would get a call that they had found three or four cars, the condition of the cars, and prices that were reasonable. Then we would have a discussion about which one of the cars we should buy. That was really my expectation when Brad and Carol left that morning to go car shopping. Boy, was I in for a surprise! Later that day I got a call from Carol saying they had bought a beautiful, well-built car. She had found a car, a Cadillac, with all the bells and whistles. Obviously, my role was greatly simplified. All I had to do was sign the papers to purchase a $45,000 Cadillac. But we made it work. It was truly Carol's car. In fact, she had not owned a car since we had traded her old Chevy Nova for my pickup truck. This car was in her name, and she claimed it as hers. It served us well for over twenty years. After Carol's stroke we never found a car as friendly for Carol as her Cadillac.

Eventually, it just wore out, but we didn't want to sell it, so we donated it to NPR.

OFF TO CUBA

Serving as dean and director of the College of Agricultural and Environmental Sciences often requires unusual travel. For me, serving in this capacity involved travel to Europe, South America, Central America, China, the Philippines, South Korea, North Korea, and Cuba.

The director for international affairs for the college was the very able Dr. Edward Kanemasu, who handled this assignment in absolutely outstanding fashion. Many of the college's international programs were funded by extramural sources, and he was exceptionally adept in securing such grants. Over the years, he had built good relations with personnel in many countries, including Cuba. In fact, he had orchestrated student exchanges with some universities in Havana.

He mentioned one day that we had been invited to visit Cuba. He followed up with the news that our spouses were also to be invited. At first, I was a bit skeptical. My first response was, "Been there, done that." I had been to Cuba—remember the hijacking? But the plan for this trip sounded like a vacation. The trip was set for Dr. Kanemasu and his wife, Karen, and Carol and me to visit Cuba sometime in the next month or so.

Since Dr. Kanemasu and his office handled all details, all Carol and I had to do was pack a bag, make sure we had a passport, and show up. Dr. Kanemasu and Karen were to fly directly to Cuba. Carol and I decided to overnight in the Bahamas. This would enable us to have a couple days of free time for a brief vacation.

Since the hotel was right on the water, we decided to go swimming. While the swimming was fun, there were sights to behold. A girl—lady—was frolicking in the water right where we were swimming. She was clothed—I should say unclothed—in what they call a thong. This provided sights we had not been brought up with. But it provided an interesting talking point for our trip.

We planned for a special dinner that evening, so we consulted the hotel concierge. He recommended a restaurant about an hour away by taxi on the other side of the island. We took him up on his recommendation and got a taxi for the most unusual ride of our life. The taxi did not have air conditioning, so all windows were down. The driver must have been in a great hurry. Since we were never able to get the windows up, Carol accepted the fact that her hair was a complete disaster. She would try to fix it once we got to the restaurant. Anyway, the dinner was superb, a great recommendation by the concierge. The taxi ride back to the hotel was just the opposite of the ride to the restaurant. The ride back was much more pleasant, with air conditioning, and the driver drove a respectable speed. All's well that ends well.

The next day we met the Kanemasus at the airport. We were both booked on the same Cubana flight from the Bahamas to Havana.

We were met at the airport by our host, who guided us around customs. We were told that we were treated just like the last US president to visit—President Jimmy Carter.

During the week we visited universities, research labs, and some government officials. For travel, Dr. Kanemasu and Karen had a Mercedes 500 SL, and Carol and I had the same kind of car.

This was a great trip, thanks to the excellent arrangements by Dr. Kanemasu. All too soon we had to head to the airport for the return trip to the US.

THE PEABODY AWARDS EVENT

The University of Georgia's Henry Grady College of Journalism and Media Communication is responsible for identifying winners and hosting a venue for presentation of the Peabody Awards. These awards are for excellence in seven categories, including news, entertainment, documentaries, children's programming, education, interactive programming, and public service. The Peabody Award winners include radio and television stations, networks, online media, producing organizations, and individuals from around the world.

The awards are presented at a luncheon in New York. Carol and I were invited to attend one of the events in the mid-'90s. The event was held at the Waldorf.

For Carol and me, it was an unusual experience to attend a luncheon with live people that we usually only saw on television. To the best of our knowledge, we didn't commit any faux pas while hobnobbing with the media celebrities.

VISITS TO OTHER MAJOR CITIES

Over our long marriage, Carol and I had the opportunity to visit several of the major cities in the US. Here are a few of the cities that we visited and related events. Without question, San Fransisco is number one. New Orleans is number two. Each of these cities are discussed elsewhere in this book.

NEW YORK—First, the Peabody Awards are already mentioned. We also attended scientific meetings as well as professional meetings while I was a professor or as undersecretary. The most enjoyable aspect of our visits was the museums and art galleries. They are fantastic. And who can forget Central Park in the middle of a great city? The dining experience at Carnegie Deli was an experience for the ages. You haven't experienced a great Reuben sandwich until you have one at Carnegie Deli. The last time we were in New York, I can't remember for what purpose, it was raining, and I left my umbrella in a taxi. Would like to have it back.

CHICAGO—It just so happened that the same time I had a professional meeting scheduled in Chicago, Riverdance was going to be performing. Carol just had to get tickets and see Riverdance. So we bought tickets almost a year ahead of the event. As it turned out, the event was not even close to being sold out. We could have bought tickets same day as the show, much cheaper and with better seats. Lesson learned.

Carol and I went up in the Sears Tower, now the Willis Tower. Unfortunately, the day we went up, it was very cloudy, so we didn't really get to see much of the advertised scenery, but we did get the trip at half price because it was so cloudy.

Carol has forgiven me for wasting half a day trying to find a restaurant that I had visited on an earlier trip. But I think a visit to the Chicago History Museum and the Field's shopping complex made up for my failed efforts to find my restaurant.

ATLANTA—While Carol never cared much for Atlanta, she loved the Fox Theatre, and of course, it is in Atlanta. Many of the university's major events, especially the black-tie ones, were held at the Fox. We always enjoyed going there. We also attended a number of productions at the Fox. Probably the single best show we ever saw there was Wagner's *The Flying Dutchman*. I still love that opera. What a show!

As dean, I authorized my staff to work with several commodity and trade groups in developing a fantastic agricultural display about Georgia agriculture for the 1996 Olympics. Our display featured several animatronic farm animals. We were told this was the first time in history that there had been such an agricultural display in the Olympics. Quite frankly, we were quite proud of the display and entertained many, many thousands of visitors. After the event the building that we had erected was purchased by the University of Georgia Griffin Campus and installed as a permanent facility there. Unfortunately, our visits during the Olympics were quite limited since I was still recovering from cancer surgery.

DALLAS—During Carol's period of interest in the classical guitar, we heard about a performance scheduled for Dallas. Since the concert was to be held on a Saturday evening, we thought we could go to Dallas on Friday evening and come back Sunday, which we did. As it turned out, for some reason that I can't remember, the concert was canceled, so we changed plans. We visited some tourist attractions in Dallas, including the botanical gardens and Cotton Bowl. This provided a great opportunity to see Dallas. On Saturday evening we visited my favorite Mexican restaurant in Dallas. While the trip did not follow the original plan, we certainly had a great time.

BIRMINGHAM—This was almost a hometown for us. While at Auburn, we visited Birmingham frequently. In fact, as a weed scientist, I had a number of experiments located in some of the highway rights-of-way within the city. Also, our daughter Judy and her family are residents of Mountain Brook, which is a suburb of Birmingham.

MEMPHIS—We made several visits to Memphis over the years. There were two or three experiences we long remembered. At the time I was serving as president of the Southern Association of Agricultural Scientists. At the annual meeting, one of the perks for the president was the largest suite in the hotel. Included in the suite was a very large room—large enough to hold a reception—and two double bedrooms.

Unfortunately, as often happens in the middle of meetings, I had to fly back to Athens overnight for some critical meeting. I would then return to Memphis for the remainder of the conference. Carol was to stay in Memphis while I was gone. The local arrangements committee, knowing we had a large reception room in our presidential suite, asked if they could borrow it for a small reception. Of course, Carol and I agreed.

A small, quiet reception it was not. Apparently, it was a very rowdy event. Of course, the host of the reception invited Carol to come and participate, but she decided just to close her bedroom door and let them party. She had many stories to tell about the rowdy reception.

The hotel was the Peabody—no relation to the Peabody Awards. One of the traditions of the hotel involves the ducks that live there. Every afternoon they are escorted to the huge fountain in the lobby for a couple of hours. The ducks are allowed to frolic in the fountain and then return to their assigned quarters on the rooftop.

What Carol and I loved most about Memphis was Charlie Vergos' Rendezvous restaurant. Arguably, they have the best ribs in the South. They are cooked in an old-fashioned brick oven that gives an aroma to the entire restaurant. We never tired of them.

TUCSON—While Tucson is not a large US city, we made several trips there. One trip in particular is noteworthy. I had meetings almost all the time, and Carol had a lot of free time. Without saying a word, one morning as I left for my conference, Carol was noncommittal about her day. She outlined several possibilities: read, relax by the pool, take a nap, et cetera.

When I returned late that evening, I was surprised. I learned that after relaxing for a few minutes that morning, Carol decided she wanted to see Mexico. So she drove our rental car to the border, parked, and walked over to Mexico. She spent the day seeing Nogales, Mexico. Apparently the trip went well, and Carol must have had a great time. As a result, she had stories to tell about her unauthorized trip to Mexico.

GALE GETS CANCER

Most of my life, I've enjoyed great health. After a routine physical, my doctor suggested that I take a test for the possibility of colon cancer. Being so busy at the office, this was something I felt like I could put off indefinitely. However, Carol had other ideas. So I took the test. The test came back indicating that I should have a colonoscopy. I knew that would take a couple of days. I just simply couldn't afford the time off from work. Besides, I was scheduled to travel to a conference in Africa. Carol's response was quick that I should make time for a colonoscopy, so I didn't fight it. My colonoscopy was immediately scheduled.

I fully expected to be back at work the day after the colonoscopy. As I was arousing from the anesthesia, I remember the doctor telling the nurse to not discharge me but to get me scheduled for surgery the next morning. Apparently, the colonoscopy had been terminated because I had such an advanced stage of colon cancer they wanted to operate immediately. I was really unhappy because the day after the surgery, I was scheduled to fly out for a conference in Cape Verde, just off the west coast of Africa. I had never been to that part of the world. I was looking forward to the visit.

When I came out of surgery, the surgeon told me that he had taken out a couple of feet of my colon and that I was good to go. After intense intravenous feeding for a week, I still recall how delicious my first bowl of Jell-O really was.

This must count as Carol being a caregiver. I'm totally confident that without her persistence, I would have just put off the initial test indefinitely until it was probably too late.

One of my brothers died very young from colon cancer. Either he did not heed the warning signs, or no one urged him to get checked.

CHAPTER 7

The Washington Experience

RETIREMENT OR JUST RETURNING TO WORK AT A DIFFERENT LOCATION

After serving in academia for thirty-five years, the last twenty-five as an agriculture administrator, it seemed to be a great time to retire. Besides, while working at the University of Georgia, I was happy, and I was generally appreciated by the administration. I had rocked a few boats in making a number of changes in the college, and there were some who expressed great pleasure at having a party to celebrate my departure. Of course, we had our new (old) house in Adel and the farm only thirty-five minutes away in North Florida. Everything was falling into place with a career done about as well as we could make it.

While these all sound like great plans, fate would have a hand in fouling up our well-laid plans for retirement.

Late one evening, well after bedtime, the phone rang. I had a call from Fred Cholick, a former colleague and agricultural dean, who was chair of the Board of Agriculture, a job I once held. He came right to the point. He said, "Would you mind if we threw your name in the hat for the position of undersecretary for Research, Education, and Economics in the US Department of Agriculture?" Carol could hear all of the conversation just about as well as I could. I reported to Fred that I would have to think it over because we had been making plans regarding our life in retirement.

THE HIRING PROCESS

This was one time I didn't have to ask Carol what she thought. She had heard the conversation completely. She volunteered that this sounded interesting and would be a great challenge for me. Carol and I both realized it would, indeed, be a very great long shot for such a position, especially as a nonpolitical type. However, in view of our apprehensions, I called Fred back the next morning and said to proceed in putting my name forward for consideration. After the phone call that morning, we thought nothing more about it for the next couple of months.

Later, I received a call from the White House's Office of Presidential Personnel indicating that I was among those being considered for a political appointment as undersecretary of agriculture in the Bush administration. They informed me that I should proceed with submitting my application. The process started with completing Form 86. While this sounds like a simple form, in reality it's exceedingly long, cumbersome, and requires a great deal of information. One part is particularly onerous for a scientist. One requirement is a list of *all* publications, which must be provided with complete, easy-to-find references. Since I have hundreds of scientific publications, this was indeed a challenge. The position also called for an FBI background check, fingerprinting, and a list of references as well. Thanks to my office staff, we pulled everything together in a couple of months, then wasted no time in getting it submitted. Then we waited, and waited, and waited, and waited some more!

THE INTERVIEW

As an administrator, I have been the interviewer for countless positions over the past couple of decades. Being the interviewee was a new experience, since I had not been a candidate for a new position since being appointed dean and director of the College of Agriculture and Environmental Sciences.

A few weeks after submitting all of my documentation, I received a call from a lady at the Office of Presidential Personnel who asked in a very pleasant voice when would be a convenient time for me to come to DC for an interview with her office. I responded quickly, and then in a minute I was scheduled for an interview.

The interview was quite pleasant. I was interviewed by two young men and two ladies who were far less than half my age. It seemed quite ironic to be interviewed by someone so young. They asked many questions. My responses provided an answer that apparently must have satisfied their queries.

I inquired about the next procedure in the process. They indicated they would brief the chief of personnel, and if everyone approved, I should then schedule an interview with the secretary of agriculture.

Now I felt like I was getting somewhere. I went straight to see the secretary. He was confident I would be approved by the Office of Presidential Personnel, so we should set up an interview in the department.

If you've ever been through a preliminary examination for a PhD, this is exactly the same kind of interview.

By this time, I was beginning to feel sufficiently confident that I called Carol and told her to start packing. After the interview with the secretary, things really seemed to be falling into place. This interview was very pleasant in that the secretary and several of his senior staff—

all political appointees—asked a lot of quite intelligent questions, especially about agriculture and my role in agriculture research.

They seemed to approve and appreciate my background and my knowledge of production agriculture as well as my scientific credentials. At the completion of this interview, the secretary indicated that things were looking good. Consequently, he recommended I start planning for a possible positive confirmation.

GETTING THE JOB

There are many steps in hiring a political appointee. Consequently, it is hard to know just when you have gotten the job. In retrospect, I learned in the process that if you don't get any negative reports at each step, you can be assured that you're still good to go for the next step in the process. After completing the interview with the secretary, I realized I had gotten positive responses from every step so far, including the application, which was approved, and the interviews by the Office of Presidential Personnel and the secretary. Even with all of these approvals by different groups, there was still one major hurdle—approval by the appropriate US Senate committee. Even with these approvals, any senator can put a hold on an appointment. As this is written, Alabama senator Tommy Tuberville is holding promotion of almost 250 US military personnel.

WHERE TO LIVE WHILE WORKING IN WASHINGTON

I don't know why, but it always seemed that I left all the dirty work to Carol when I started a new job. While she was planning the move, I thought I would identify a few possible living sites so we both could then consider them before we made our new home in the Washington area. First, I was shocked—decent apartments in the Washington area started at $3,500–$5,000 per month. Even though Amber our cat was advanced in years, she would be welcome in some apartments—for a fee. Carol had to fly to DC so that we could select our apartment. We settled on a beautiful, nice apartment on the fourteenth floor of the Meridian, one of the nicest apartments in Arlington, Virginia. It was directly across the street from the headquarters for the National Science Foundation. For Amber the fee was only thirty-five dollars per month. Wish we could have stayed that cheap.

The location was fantastic—every kind of restaurant you could imagine was within walking distance, the Metro could be reached without even crossing a street, and there was a huge vertical shopping center just across the street. At about this time, I was officially notified I had the job pending approval by the US Senate confirmation hearing. Carol had returned home (Adel) and had finalized the moving contract, closed the house in Adel, and caught another plane back to Washington. Even though we had made great plans to bring Amber with us, things didn't work out. Amber was certainly an elderly cat by any measure, and she just didn't want to fly on an airplane, so she decided she would go ahead and finish her life here on this earth and decided not to go with us to Washington.

GETTING SETTLED

In the anticipation that I would be the successful candidate, earlier I had bought a small car, a Toyota, rather than taking our big sedan to DC. Since Carol was handling all the housekeeping details regarding the move and setting up housekeeping, I concentrated on getting oriented to my new job. Unfortunately, until you are confirmed by the US Senate, you cannot go into your new office. However, you can begin working unofficially out of a conference room or someone else's office until you are confirmed by the Senate.

Preparation for this event is a serious matter that is of concern to the secretary. Certainly, the secretary and the entire department want the confirmation hearing to always be successful and to proceed without incident. Consequently, each political appointee must be processed by the department's "murder board." Such a board is convened by the deputy secretary and includes the most politically savvy people in the department. The purpose is to throw every possible question they can think of at you and see how you respond. Again, much like the prelims for a PhD. Since I did OK with the murder board, the secretary felt confident in working with the Senate staff to schedule a hearing. In fact, the department had four political appointees to be considered in my class. The one thing I learned that was drilled over and over is that a member of Congress can ask anything—absolutely anything—they wish to ask. On the other hand, an appointee doesn't have to answer the question; however, it is absolutely imperative that you *respond* to their question in an intelligent, rational, and logical manner.

The confirmation hearings went well. Having both the chair (Senator Saxby Chambliss, R-GA) and ranking member (Senator Tom Harkin, D-IA) of the agriculture committee know you personally really made it quite an enjoyable experience for me. After the Senate approved, I was sworn in that very afternoon by the secretary. Carol attended the swearing in ceremony conducted by the secretary.

Now I could go to my office and start to work? Nooooo, nooooo! I had just learned that the senior senator from Nevada had put a hold on all political appointees in the USDA because of an issue regarding a concern about an ARS laboratory in his state. Until that issue was addressed by the USDA Agricultural Research Service, all appointees were on hold. This hold lasted for a couple weeks. Unfortunately, as soon as the Nevada senator released his hold, the junior senator from Louisiana put on another hold, which held up our confirmation for another week. Eventually, all holds were released, and I could get into my office and officially start to work.

Meanwhile, Carol was getting the apartment livable: getting a TV service, computer service, and other needs to ensure our creature comforts.

LIVING IN THE DC AREA

I can only share a very few of the highlights of our life in the Washington, DC, area. Our apartment was actually in Arlington, Virginia, just across the river from DC. First, we never counted, but there must have been fifteen or twenty great restaurants within easy walking distance of our apartment. This included a great Chinese restaurant that was Carol's favorite. Of course, a short Metro ride opened up countless more restaurants. Also, we found something to do about every weekend. We saw museums, art galleries, and so many other things in DC, including the US National Arboretum, Botanical Garden, and many other sites.

One of the most enjoyable things we often did was to visit Old Town, Alexandria. After a couple of visits, we learned to get off the Metro and walk the entire length of King Street all the way to the torpedo factory, now an art complex, on the river. You could see a multitude of stores, shops, vendors, and so many things on this walk. Of course, the church where Robert E. Lee had attended services was a nice place to visit. We often managed to have lunch at a restaurant in the wharf area that had a fantastic buffet that always included caviar. I am still searching for a buffet restaurant in the South that has caviar on their salad bar.

Without question, one of our favorite places to visit was the Kennedy Center. We saw many, many great plays, musical performances, and other cultural activities. In fact, we joked among ourselves that all of our money was spent at the Kennedy Center because we couldn't resist the many great activities and performances. The Kennedy Center offered a wide range of entertainment—something for everyone.

CAROL GETS TICKETS FOR ME
TO SEE WONDER WOMAN

It is impossible to discuss the Kennedy Center and not mention one of the nicest things Carol ever did for me. She knew that I have long been a fan of Wonder Woman, a.k.a. Lynda Carter. Well, Carol noticed in a Kennedy Center flyer that Lynda Carter was scheduled for a one-night performance at the center. Carol got me a ticket for a choice seat and put it on my schedule to attend the performance. She was going to stay home for my "boy's night out" with Lynda Carter.

I was not disappointed. Many women have played Wonder Woman, but none could come close to being as good as Lynda Carter. Folks, while she is a great actress as Wonder Woman, she can really sing. She put on a great performance.

What more could a loving wife do for a husband?

CAROL SEES THE QUEEN

In 2007, soon after Carol made it possible for me to see Lynda Carter, she learned that Queen Elizabeth II was coming to America from the United Kingdom. In only a few days, information was released regarding the queen's itinerary. She was going to visit the White House as one of the venues. There would be a limited number of opportunities for the public to attend and see the queen.

As you can imagine, Carol immediately decided she just had to see the queen—up close. I don't recall the exact process, but Carol was able to get an invitation for the queen's visit to the White House.

As soon as her invitation was validated, Carol started planning. Of course, the number one issue was what to wear. She soon settled on yellow—her (and my) favorite color. The event was during the workday, so I was totally out of the picture. Carol would take the Metro and handle all of the related details.

For me, there was not much of a story, but for Carol, well, she talked about seeing the queen for months and months. I'm quite confident that if Carol were here today, she would say seeing the queen was probably the single most important highlight during her Washington years. For Carol, seeing the queen was quite comparable to me seeing Lynda Carter.

SPECIAL EVENTS AND ACTIVITIES

Carol greatly enjoyed exploring the Washington area by herself during the week. She became quite adept at managing bus routes and transportation schedules. She found many interesting programs and activities at the Kennedy Center and the array of museums and art galleries. Also, there were frequently special programs and displays at the botanical gardens and the National Arboretum. She especially enjoyed the arboretum because it was a part of the Agricultural Research Service, one of the units in the Research, Education, and Economics mission area. This was an area that I had responsibility for.

Cherry blossom time is a great time to visit DC. The cherry blossoms are one of the world's most beautiful displays of nature. The beautiful cherry blossoms and the hordes of people around the tidal basin make one proud to be an American. My takeaway is this: I would encourage every American citizen, if at all possible, to visit Washington, the nation's capital, at least once during their life, preferably during cherry blossom time.

It was certainly an honor for me to have the opportunity of working in our nation's capital. I could sit in my office and look out the window to see the Washington Monument.

Fourth of July fireworks were a real treat. The deputy secretary invited the senior staff in the department to an informal party on the roof of the Whitten Building to watch the fireworks display on the Fourth of July. I don't know if they still do this. It is not often recognized that the only department of the US government that has headquarters directly on the Mall is the Department of Agriculture. The department headquarters is located in the Whitten Building.

Carol enjoyed the dress-up affairs much more than I did. I think this was because she always looked nice, and I always felt out of place.

Another quite enjoyable experience was attending the orchid show at the US National Arboretum. What a sight to see some of the most beautiful orchids in the world—all in one place. Another great event was the National Book Festival put on by First Lady Laura Bush. Carol bought a congressional cookbook at one of these events.

It's a pity space will not allow me to relate more of our experiences while living in the DC area. Truly, the Washington sojourn was personally the high point of my career, but more importantly, it provided some of the most enjoyable moments of our marriage. We never tired of strolling through the arboretum, museums, art galleries, and botanical gardens. Who could ever get tired of strolling through the Eastern Market, one of the oldest open-air markets in America, dating back to the beginning of our country?

CAROL'S PENCHANT FOR HELPING OTHERS

One of Carol's attributes was a big heart. She was always touched by those in need. While she liked to help people, she assiduously avoided recognition for anything she did for others. Now, after her death, I'm still trying to thin down the organizations that she had contributed to in the past.

I first tried to respond by indicating that she was deceased, but that simply did not work. So what I try to do now is focus on those charitable organizations that I knew she had special interest in. I continue to make a small contribution on her behalf.

While she had a big heart for helping people by making contributions, she always got very exasperated that as soon as she had made a contribution, she received another request. I tried to explain that these organizations assume that the best source of a new contribution comes from those who have already made a contribution. That never seemed to satisfy Carol. She seemed to think if you made one contribution, that should last for a little while anyway.

Soon after we relocated to the Washington, DC, area, Carol went to the commissary at Fort Myer for groceries. At the checkout, the lady in front of her had a couple of kids and a baby, along with a huge buggy full of groceries. Carol overheard the conversation between the lady and the cashier. Apparently, the lady was having an exceedingly bad day and had forgotten her checkbook. The cashier was quite adamant that she was not allowed to give credit to anyone. The lady was in a dilemma. Carol stepped in and handed the cashier her American Express card and said, "Put her groceries on my card." The cashier told Carol, "You might not get your money back." According to Carol, her response was to just smile. Later that evening she told me what she had done. I told her exactly what the cashier had told her. Carol then smiled at me. Carol soon got a check and a very nice note of thanks and appreciation from the lady.

In the years following Carol's stroke, shopping became exceedingly difficult. Consequently, for most graduations, weddings, birthdays, and other events that called for presents, Carol simply used a check for a gift. This seemed to work, but after her death, I've had to consult with my children to determine what size check they should receive from me for their birthday. Unfortunately, occasionally I have suspected they might've inflated their expectation. Of course, Carol would be pleased.

Carol's penchant for helping others didn't just stop with people. It included all of God's creatures—especially birds. I would like to give myself a pat on the back. After Carol's first stroke, she used the family living room as her exercise room where her exercise machine was located. This room has a huge picture window. I thought having a bird feeder in front of a big window just might be a positive thing for helping Carol, as she spent considerable time each day on the exercise machine.

As it turns out, this was a great idea because birds flocked to the bird feeders in droves. It simply lifted Carol's spirits. During the exercise activity, she was on the machine twice a day—every day. She had an absolutely unobstructed view of the birds that flocked to the feeder. Even when I pointed out that the birds were sometimes naughty and ate my figs and grapes as well as my blueberries, she always said they were hungry and needed the fruit more than I did. Her day would be made absolutely complete if a redbird came to get his daily allowance of food. In fact, if a redbird came, it would be worth a phone call to me in the office, which I always enjoyed receiving.

Simple things like seeing a redbird at the feeder and acknowledging our responsibility in caring for God's creatures made loving Carol so easy and wonderful.

Now, a year after Carol's death, the birds are still being taken care of. I don't even fuss when they eat my figs, grapes, or blueberries. Carol always said that God notices when we take care of his creatures. Our tombstone, located in the Hickory Grove Cemetery, features, on Carol's side, a picture of a beautiful red bird, and on my side, a picture of one of the world's worst weeds—purple nutsedge.

CHAPTER 8

The Stroke Years

VALENTINE'S DAY 2015

On this particular weekend, I went down to the farm on Friday. Carol was to come down the next morning, and we would share the weekend together. I was awakened early in the morning on Valentine's Day 2015 by the jarring ring of my iPhone. My son Brad called and said his mother was in the emergency room. Having arisen from a deep sleep, I'm not sure how I responded or what I said, but from the tone of his voice, I knew it was serious. He said she was in the emergency room at South Georgia Medical Center in Valdosta. I dressed as quickly as possible and headed for the hospital.

Most of the day was spent not knowing just how serious Carol's situation was. Brad filled me in on the details of getting her to the hospital.

Eventually, we learned she had had a stroke—primarily in a region of the brain often associated with diabetes. When she was stabilized, we were allowed to see her for a brief visit. We soon learned that her left side was almost completely paralyzed. There were other complications, including slurred speech. We had many questions but few real answers. One of the first positive things we learned was that the region of her brain not related to the paralysis and speech was not affected.

As she continued to improve, the doctors started discussing therapy. While their comments were always quite professional, they were just a bit optimistic. They were careful not to give us false hope but always encouraged us to remain positive. After a week or so in the hospital, Carol began intense speech therapy, then therapy for her arm and leg. The first positive signs were improvements in speech. That obviously gave us some hope that maybe her arm and leg would improve as well. The hospital was scheduled to release Carol either to home or to an assisted living facility.

MOVING TO AN ASSISTED LIVING FACILITY

Wanting the best care for Carol, we agreed that a few months in an assisted living home would be best. I selected an assisted living facility located in Tifton. This would allow me to go the office for an hour or so each day, leaving me then free to stay with Carol. Living in such a facility enabled more convenient therapy treatments.

The time spent in the assisted living facility helped Carol, but I was learning how the staff helped her so I could take over when we had to go home. One thing that intrigued me was how Carol could get a bath. The staff at the assisted living facility simply put her in a wheelchair and rolled her into a shower. I knew I could do better.

While we had hoped that Carol was going to be complete again, we finally came to realize that this was probably not to be. Her disability was a new normal and permanent.

The assisted living facility had several positive things going for it. First, the food was quite good. Also, it was a very pleasant environment.

COMING HOME

After a few months in the assisted living facility, she was discharged and released for home care. Now, I was officially her caregiver. Many will not believe it, but I was truly frightened—could I be successful in taking care of the most important person in the world to me? I recalled some of the earlier challenges in my life where I was unsure of approaches and actions. I committed myself to doing the best I could.

Brad was my steadfast helper. First, our bed required modifications, which he handled in fine fashion. It had to be a precise height to facilitate Carol getting in and out. Fortunately, several years earlier we had installed a walk-in shower. Brad installed grab bars around the shower as well as for all the toilets in the house. By now, it was the end of summer, and we were looking forward to Thanksgiving at the farm.

THE FALL

Thanksgiving was always a very special day for our family. Brad and his family were coming to the farm to join us for the long weekend. Brad and I were going to do some farm work and then smoke the turkey and prepare dressing and all the trimmings for Thanksgiving dinner.

Our house on the farm has a large back porch, but it is ground level. It has several steps down from the main part of the house. Something was going on on the back porch, and Carol wanted to join in the fun. In a few minutes, I learned a very valuable lesson in being a caregiver.

There was a good, strong handrail on the right side of the steps down to the porch. This was on the side of Carol's strong arm. Consequently, she was able to navigate the steps without any problems. Soon, whatever was going on was completed, and it was time to go back inside the house. As a result, Carol turned around and started to go back up the stairs. Unfortunately, this time the handrail was on her left, matching her stroke-weakened left arm. I immediately took her right hand but didn't give any thought. Of course, the left arm was no help in gripping the handrail. As a result, she lost balance and started to fall. Since I had not been prepared, she easily slipped out of my hand, and I didn't hold her because I was not mentally prepared. For her fall, I totally blame myself, even though Carol never blamed me. I know in my heart I had failed her as her caregiver.

As her caregiver, I should have been aware of the situation that led to her fall. At the moment, though, there was little time for recriminations, because as soon as Carol fell, she shrieked with pain. Obviously, this was a very nasty fall, and she was in constant pain for a long time. Immediately after she fell, Brad called 911 for an ambulance. While it seemed like an eternity, the ambulance arrived in only twelve to fifteen minutes, which is very quick for our remote location in the country. All this time, Carol was in excruciating pain. It was even worse when the paramedics worked to get her on a stretcher so they could get her into the ambulance. After getting her in the ambulance, they tried to deal with the pain and then transported her to the South Georgia Medical Center in Valdosta. We followed.

Late that afternoon the surgeon told us that the bones in her hip, including the femur, were not just broken but shattered—the surgeon's words. Immediate surgery was required and completed later that night.

Even with this trauma, Carol maintained a positive attitude. She was to remain in the hospital for less than a week. I was advised by the hospital staff to identify a nursing home for an extended period. Keep in mind since Carol's stroke, I had been making decisions about her care with never enough information to be comfortable. Again, I did the best that I could and hoped for a favorable outcome.

There was a nursing home directly across the street from the hospital. I reasoned that being close to the hospital would be best. Consequently, within a week after the fall, we would move Carol into a nursing home—across from the hospital.

THE NURSING HOME

As soon as Carol was moved into the nursing home, we both tried to make this new arrangement work. We had a semiprivate room. I quickly noticed that Carol was the only person in the nursing home whose caregiver stayed with her all the time. Of course, I had done that in the assisted living facility, but there we had a private room. I observed that the staff was totally overworked and that Carol, a patient, was totally dependent on the overworked staff. Probably the greatest advantage of my presence was, I think, that it encouraged the staff to take a bit more interest and care for Carol. All this time, I was observing the way the staff did things for Carol. I knew that eventually I would have total responsibility for Carol's welfare.

While I stayed with Carol almost every day, I didn't try to entertain her. I would work some, read newspapers, talk a little with Carol, run an occasional errand. I was just there. I felt so sorry for her roommate, whose husband would drop by maybe once a week. But even those visits with his wife were apparently not very pleasant, because it seemed all they did was fuss.

Did I say that almost as soon as we got settled in the nursing home, we began to plan and plot our escape? We just knew that if we could ever get out of the nursing home into our real home, life would be a bit better. Carol was taking therapy, but we knew now that the paralysis was permanent, as we had suspected earlier. The new normal would never be anything like the old normal.

After a few weeks, we tried to get a private room. Eventually, we were lucky. Finally, about three weeks before we left, Carol was able to get into a private room. This made life 100 percent better.

Our experience in the nursing home caused Carol to have a fear of ever having to return to such a facility. Consequently, I reverently prayed that if it was God's will that he would let me live just one day longer than Carol so I could take care of her until the end of her life. God answered that prayer—now that I've lived longer than Carol. I am forever grateful for God answering that prayer. I'm ready whenever my life is no longer needed on this earth.

ADAPTING TO LIFE WITH A DISABILITY

Since the time between the assisted living facility and Thanksgiving was only a very few months, we hardly had time to establish a routine. Now with the hip problem behind us, as well as the stroke, we set about starting to establish our new normal. I'm pleased to say after the fall at Thanksgiving, Carol never had such a fall for the remainder of her life. She did have one occasion when she lost balance, kind of crumpled up, and ended up on the floor, but it was not a fall. For that I am exceedingly grateful. I think it's because she learned a great deal about how to take care of herself. Most importantly she never ever got in a hurry.

My job was to always be vigilant of obstacles. Even in church, I always tried to walk close to her to protect her from a running child.

I was really glad that she and Brad had bought the Cadillac, because it was the easiest car we had for her getting in and out. Oh, how Carol wanted to drive. She must have asked me ten thousand times to let her drive, but I never relented. I could just see her stroke-weakened left leg getting tangled up in preventing her other leg from getting to the brake, which would be a disaster. I had taken my earlier failure as a caregiver to heart and realized it was *my* responsibility to not ever to put her in danger. Same with the kitchen. I would let her use the microwave but never use the stove burners or an oven. I tried, Lord I tried, to keep stuff off the floor in the house. I quickly learned that the biggest job of a caregiver is to make the world safe for your patient. Also, you have to maintain vigilance at all times.

Even after returning home, Carol would be engaged in various degrees of exercise for the remainder of her life. We tried to put as positive a spin as possible on her exercising. For example, I jokingly told Carol repeatedly to use the middle finger on her stroke-weakened left arm to measure progress. Eventually, she was able to use that finger to offer an obscene gesture.

There is absolutely no doubt the stroke brought Carol and me closer together. We had a great marriage before the stroke and an even better marriage after the stroke. The stroke did nothing but strengthen our love for each other. You will notice I haven't mentioned depression in the last couple of chapters. For some reason it seems depression became less of a problem for Carol in later years.

THE LIFE OF A CAREGIVER

Over my life, I have accumulated several titles, including mister, professor, doctor (PhD type), lieutenant, captain, major, lieutenant colonel, colonel, commandant, dean, director, chief scientist, undersecretary, unexpected chef, and retiree, but the title I truly cherish is that of caregiver. While all these titles, with the exception of caregiver, are enjoyed by many, the title of caregiver is, indeed, a very special title for those who earn it.

When Carol experienced her first stroke in 2015, I was immediately given the title of caregiver—an unearned and quite undeserved title at the time. The first true caregivers Carol experienced were at the hospital, then at the assisted living facility, and finally the nursing home. After she was released from the nursing home, I had to become a caregiver for Carol. While I now had the title, it took a catastrophic failure on my part to really start earning the title and learning how to be a real caregiver.

The catastrophic event described in a previous section—the fall—happened a short time after leaving the assisted living facility. While I offered my hand, which was a proper gesture, it was just not effective. She lost her balance quickly and easily slipped out of my hand. The fall was extremely devastating.

While it is true I offered her my hand, I was not mentally aware of the situation. While Carol never once blamed me, I knew immediately that I had failed miserably as her caregiver.

This event helped me to become a real caregiver. I now realized that being a caregiver involved much more than just doing things—it required mental awareness at all times. For example, steps, stairs, or any unusual situation must be carefully evaluated before attempting to negotiate. Always think ahead. And always be mentally alert!

With a strong-willed patient, it is not always easy to say no, but as a real caregiver, you must always resist. If for some reason it becomes impossible to resist, then the caregiver must take extraordinary precautions and exercise exceptional care in observing the situation. The caregiver must never allow the patient to be in a situation where there is the possibility of danger.

For a caregiver, there is much to learn. As a man I often wondered why it took so long for Carol to get dressed. After helping her dress a few times, it became quite understandable why women take so long to get ready to go somewhere.

A new caregiver has much to learn. I learned many tricks and ideas that were very helpful. While I never mastered the act of fixing Carol's natural hair to her satisfaction, I did learn one very important aspect of managing hair. That lesson was hair must be brushed every single day—no exception or days off. I soon learned that tangles only get worse each day. After the first episode of tangles, we had to go to a hair salon. I never did let her tangles become so serious again.

Since I could not fix her natural hair to her satisfaction, she always insisted on wearing a wig when we went out in public. Not to brag, but I got pretty efficient in selecting wigs. Of course, I always had considerable input in purchasing wigs. I also mastered the art of pinning up her natural hair to facilitate the installation of the wig.

Baths were always a lot of fun for me. Having a huge walk-in shower greatly facilitated giving Carol a bath. Her favorite part of the bath was, without question, the long shampoo. She really enjoyed my nimble fingers in giving her a long shampoo.

Learning to buy ladies' stuff was another real challenge. Occasionally, she would ask me to take her shopping, but it was always difficult. She came to depend on me to shop for her. For clothes, I learned to find a lady that was just about Carol's size and ask her to help in finding items. I would simply say, "My wife is about your size, and if it fits you, it will fit her." I learned label sizes are often meaningless for

ladies' clothes. Usually, that process worked. I learned there are countless items that women need that men have never heard of—such things
as eyebrow pencils—and they come in countless sizes and colors. I had
to learn to first find where they are in the store and then how to select
the precise item Carol needed. And these items are not cheap. I also
learned that in many clothing stores, there are limited staff. When
asking for help from a customer, be sure to ask only older ladies. If you
ask a young lady for help, oftentimes they will think you're just hitting
on them. Most older ladies were often very helpful and appreciative of
being able to help.

Because becoming a caregiver is quite similar in many ways to each
new job you undertake, it's always a learning experience. The major
difference is there is no room for mistakes. I know I learned from my
mistakes and vowed never to make the same mistakes again.

The only big difference is the reward from being a caregiver is un-
imaginable. Often when Carol and I disagreed on a safety precaution,
she always knew I had her best interest at heart.

Being Carol's caregiver was one of the true highlights of my life. I
enjoyed every minute of helping her make the best of her life. That is
why we always prayed that I would live just one day longer than she,
so that I could take care of her all of her natural life. I thank God for
answering that prayer.

NOVEMBER 5, 2022

Even before the stroke, we spent most of our weekends at the farm.
While I had inherited a portion of our father's farm, there was no
house on our part of the property. However, after the death of one of
my brothers who did have a house, Carol and I were able to negotiate
the rental and eventual purchase of the house.

As a result, we usually went to the farm each weekend. This
would allow us to work in the yard or on the farm and enjoy country living and attend church where I grew up. We would return
home after church each Sunday. Attending church was very im-

portant to us, and we loved our church family. This weekend was no different from most any other weekend. We decided to drive down from Adel on Saturday morning, have lunch, and maybe rake a few leaves and relax.

One thing I remember about Saturday night was that Carol was looking through her chest of drawers and ran across an old Sunday school book. She hollered out, and I ran to see the problem. She had found several crisp twenty-dollar bills stuck in her Sunday school book. She immediately exclaimed, "This is an omen." She said she would put half in the shoebox at church for the shoebox ministry,[1] and the other half was to go to another good cause. Unfortunately, I have forgotten what she was going to do with the other half of the money. The shoebox ministry is featured in great detail the next section of this book. If I can ever remember what was to be done with the other half of the newfound money, I will follow through with her wishes. Until then I guess I will just leave the money tucked in her Sunday school book until I pass on. That donation to the shoebox ministry was to be the last act of helping others in Carol's life.

NOVEMBER 6, 2022

Sunday morning was always a very busy time for us. We had a strict schedule that enabled us to seldom be late for Sunday school and church. We always had a light breakfast—careful to save at least an hour for dressing prior to Sunday school. Even after the stroke, Carol was able to do her personal hygiene and apply makeup. My responsibility was to make sure I had packed appropriate church outfits, along with proper shoes and knee-highs, and never, ever forget a wig. I never got cleared for fixing her natural hair even though I tried repeatedly. She was able to "fix" her face. I would get dressed while

---

1 The shoebox ministry is an effort to pack a regular shoebox with miscellaneous items for those in need in Haiti.

she was doing this in order to then help her get dressed. Of course, the big challenge was to get the wig just right. Usually, we had ample time and a few free minutes to spare. It was only a four- or five-minute drive to church.

The church had never built a handicap ramp. After Carol's stroke, the church immediately set about building a beautiful ramp to enable Carol to easily enter and exit the church. They even added a nice roof over the ramp after we got drenched a couple of times getting into church. Carol was forever grateful for the church building these facilities.

As usual, we were on time for Sunday school. The main service immediately followed Sunday school. This was the first Sunday of the month, so we all shared communion. While the congregation went down to the altar to take communion, our minister, Steve McHargue, always graciously brought the bread and wine to Carol. Another kind gesture that Carol truly appreciated and that made her feel just a bit special.

As church ended, Carol said she must put her money in the shoebox for the shoebox ministry. So we gingerly made our way to the church vestibule. As usual, I followed, trying to walk as closely behind her as I possibly could to protect her from someone inadvertently bumping into her or a small child in a hurry to get out of the church.

We reached the table with the collection shoebox and a stack of *The Upper Room*s. Carol retrieved a copy of *The Upper Room* and gave it to me, then proceeded to put the folded bills into the shoebox. As she was pushing the bills down through the slot, she fell back into my arms since I was immediately behind her. I looked down and saw her stroke-weakened left leg was totally askew. I said something to Carol about helping her to straighten her leg but got no response. Now she was totally in my arms, and I was unable to hold her much longer.

I quickly called Stephen Williams, a cousin, to help me hold Carol. He is very strong and immediately responded to my call. He took my place holding Carol. That freed me to run to the car and retrieve the wheelchair. While getting Carol to the car, she was totally unresponsive. Several of us were able to get her in the car.

My first plan was to drive straight to the hospital in Valdosta. But before we could do anything, several of us realized things were far more serious. As a result of this recognition, one of the members of the church family called 911 for an ambulance. We simply tried to watch Carol for the next ten minutes until the ambulance arrived.

As soon as a paramedic saw Carol, she made a quick assessment and said that we needed to take a Life Flight to the best stroke center in the area, which was Tallahassee Memorial Hospital in Tallahassee, Florida. Consequently, the ambulance took Carol to a landing zone a short distance from the church in Lee, Florida, for the flight to Tallahassee Memorial Hospital. Stephen drove me to the hospital. His wife, Jennifer, followed him so that Stephen would have a way home.

Carol never regained consciousness from the beginning of the stroke in the vestibule of the church. Death did not occur until later that evening. Her last conscious thought had occurred as she fell into my arms. When Carol and I married, I promised to love her until death parted us. Death was the only thing that could separate us, and on November 6, 2022, it did. I will continue to love Carol until I take my last breath and we meet in our heavenly home. After offering any tissues from Carol's body that might be useful for others, I watched as Carol was taken off the ventilator and died peacefully.

While Carol's death was a great personal loss, I am reminded of the great joy and meaning she brought to my life. She had a great impact on her family and many friends. I think the opening statement in the book says it all. While she faced many obstacles in her life, she did not allow them to dictate her destiny. One only has to read her poetry to get a glimpse of her indomitable spirit.

The end.

Tombstone for Gale and Carol

Carol's Poetry

Leaves
are their
most brilliant
right before
they die
I want
to be
like a
leaf

Eva Carol Jones Buchanan

MY LIFE'S ESSENTIALS

A close relationship with the Lord
Cool, fresh water to drink
Healthy food—but not too much
Loving family and friends
My walker and stick (for reaching, grabbing, and picking up)
Word Seek and Scrabble
The sun by day and the moon and stars by night
(I trust they are still shining)
A cup of coffee
Insulin
Birds singing
An occasional piece of chocolate
You!

WHAT IS A MAN?

A man is secure in his God-given masculinity.
A man is strong in his convictions.
A man is confident he can lead, advise, and guide.
A man is caring and not ashamed of shedding a tear.
You are a man!

LITTLE THINGS ARE MOMENTOUS

When you rearrange my pillow, I notice.
When you leave a reminder that a man has been here,
I laugh with delight.
When you touch my hand and pat my back, the feeling lingers.
When you sing, I am happier than when listening to birds.
When you try to redirect my thinking, I ponder.
It's the little things about you I love.

THE LORD IS MOVING

The Lord is moving over the land.
He looks for us with outstretched hand.
When He saw the state His world was in,
He knew He'd have to cleanse our sin.

He endured the cross in our place,
Thus redeeming us by His grace.
He'd left His perfect home above,
And all He asks from us is love.

WHERE ARE YOU?

I miss you. I long to have you near me.
I long to converse with you. Then I realized:
There are no ducks in the desert.
(But read Isaiah 43:19)

IF

If you need a friend,
I am here.
If you feel someone is thinking
of you,
you are always on my mind.
If you want someone to hold your hand,
mine longs to touch you.
If you are feeling low,
remember the joy you bring to me.
If you wish to be unconditionally loved,
I already do.

CHOICES

If I had to choose between
singing like an angel
or loving you,
I'd never sing again.

If I could walk, run,
and dance with delight
or love you,
I'd never walk unaided.

If I once again could play
my guitar and the piano
or love you,
I'd never pick up another instrument.

If I could behold the moon and stars
and the ocean waves and sand
or love you,
I'd be forever confined to my room.

God knows the choices
for our lives.

LISTEN TO THE WIND

Listen to the wind blow.
Though we are apart,
You may hear a whisper
Coming from my heart.

It will say you're precious,
Worth more than anything.
It will say I love you.
So hear my lone heart sing.

Listen to the wind talk.
I hope it makes you smile,
For here below we know such joy
Lasts only for a while.

LIFE'S MYSTERIES

Can you count every leaf
on a large oak tree?
Then you know how often I
think of you.

Can you weigh all the waters
in Earth's oceans, rivers, and seas?
Then you know the depth of
my feelings for you.

Can you see every grain of sand
in the ocean's beach?
Then you know every wish and prayer
I have for your happiness.

Can you name every star in
the universe?
Then you know the vastness of
my love for you.

Ah, the mysteries of life.

AFTER CHRISTMAS

Santa has gone.
The tree is down.
But take heart—
do not despair.

The love and joy
That Jesus brings
Remain for all times
everywhere.

HAPPY BIRTHDAY

I thank God you were born
on this date.
I thank God you are now
in my life.
You inspire me—
to be a better person
to be grateful for all my blessings
to think happy thoughts
to show my love
Happy birthday!

HAPPY BIRTHDAY!

Though we cannot be together
on this special day, you
are still in my thoughts
and in my heart.
I love you.

WEATHER

I am affected by the weather.
When there is sunshine, blue skies,
and singing birds,
it is easy to feel
carefree and gay.

But when rain clouds come
and all is gray,
I must remember to
think of you.

This restores my spirit.
I feel happiness.
I feel hope.
I feel love.
Let it rain!

HAPPY EASTER

What's wrong with the weather?
It's too hot, too dry, too cold,
too wet.
Rejoice—He is risen!

I need money for my car, for food,
for my family.
Rejoice—He is risen!

My work is too hard. There are
not enough hours in the day.
Rejoice—He is risen!

I am bored. The days are long.
Nothing ever happens.
Rejoice—He is risen!

There are wars and rumors
of wars.
Rejoice—He is risen!

I want a friend, companionship,
love.
Rejoice—He is risen!

HOPE IS...

the mother bird nudging her
fledgling out of the nest
for its first flight.

the family member nursing her
loved one through illness.

the workers investing for
the future.

the farmer planting seeds
in the spring.

the person loving unconditionally.

THE CHAPEL

I come to the chapel
To seek peace of mind.
Only my present and past
Do I find.

The pulpit, the organ,
Stained glass windows, and altar—
The hymnals, the pews,
At them all I now falter.

Oh, God, forgive me,
I'm not what I should be.
There's so much I want.
And even more that I could be.

A thought calms me now
Like the soft setting sun:
It's making the best
Of what I've become.

Take what I'm doing,
And make something of it.
Take what I want,
Let me rise up above it.

Callaway Gardens
7-15-81

LAUREL SPRINGS TRAIL

Shady, secluded,
uphill and down.
Rocks, pine straw,
A rustling sound.
A black snake, ants,
a bird in the trees.
The brook, the trail,
The sun and the breeze.
Shady, secluded,
uphill and down.
Pebbles, wildflowers—
a haven I've found.

MARINATED ARTICHOKE HEARTS

Old movies at 2:00 or 3:00
In the morning—
A bag of Hershey's kisses
all to myself—
And marinated artichoke hearts.

Now you know my quirky
compulsions.
What are your marinated
artichoke hearts?

CREATIVITY

How can we communicate with the
depths of our minds? Everything great—every
piece of music, work of art, book or play; every
architectural structure, space launch, dance, or poem—
was once an idea in someone's mind.

Perhaps we each have the necessary
chemistry within our brains to create infinite
ideas, but we have not learned to reach into
our subconscious and experiment with the
unfamiliar properties there.

Is it by practice, or by chance, that we
recognize an idea or feeling as novel or exciting?

WILD BIRD SEED

Have you ever had a good idea like
scattering wild bird seed in winter, but put it off
from day to day?

Sometimes I wish I could die. But
then I think that maybe God does care, and
like me and the bird seed, when He has the
time, He'll send me a sign.

So I scatter seed outside my window,
and wait for you.

I LOVE YOU, OK?

When all else seems futile—
dreams were only dreams, hopes were only
hopes, even the person I might have been
was only the person I might have been—
then let me escape to a hidden corner of
my heart and find someone there.

Let me say I love you.
And you say OK.

THOUGHTS AT FDR PARKWAY

What is it about a place that makes us want to scoop up
bits and pieces of it (like rocks, shells, leaves, or
flowers) and take them back to someone as if
we could transport our feelings like
souvenirs?

It's not the place. It's the person with whom we
wish to share our happiness.

THE SUMMER IN THE SOUTH

The summer in the South.
The hot, hot summer in the South.

You are the shade tree on the edge
of the parched field.
You are the dark rain cloud that
appears after a four-week drought.
You are the cool water going down
my dry throat.
You are the breeze across my face
as I hang sheets on the clothesline.

The hot, hot summer in the South.

STAY WITH ME

Maybe I'm not long for this world;
or maybe I'll live forever.
Whichever, I want you with me
all the way.

Maybe I'm not easy to get along with;
or maybe I'm fun and loving,
Whichever, I want you with me
all the way.

HOW CAN I SING WITHOUT YOU?

I want to sing.
But you are my song.

I want to write.
But you are my story.

I want to live.
But you are my life.

How can I sing without you?

WHY DO I LOVE THEE?
LET ME COUNT THE WAYS*

1. I am awestruck by your countenance.
2. I am excited by your masculinity.
3. Your virility astounds me.
4. I admire your strength.
5. You have an incredible spirit.
6. I applaud your courage.
7. I am envious of your enthusiasm.
8. I am amazed by your vitality.
9. I am humbled by your caring nature.
10. Your smile delights me.

Why Do I Love Thee?
Because You're You!

*My apologies to Elizabeth Barrett Browning
and her "How Do I Love Thee?"

YOU ARE ALL AROUND ME

You are all around me.

I see you in the cloud floating above me.
As it changes shape, you turn from a
stellar image into an even more
fascinating vision.

I see you in the squirrel who
cannot sit still. He scurries along,
investigating his surroundings.

You are the bird seeking me as he
perches first on the fence, then
on the tree limb and on to the
bird feeder. He, too, is in
constant motion as he flicks his
tail and twitches his beak. I feel
loved as he sings songs of joy
for me.

Lastly, I see you in the rose,
God's most perfect plant of desire.

Yes, you are all around me.

MY HERO

Inside every great man is a boy,
and once you have found him he never
leaves your heart.

He exaggerates. He pontificates.
Yet he is not aware of his own true
glory.

He needs you. He needs to be
held close with love.

A PSALM

Oh, Lord, I tremble at your
power.

You are the Creator. That alone
makes you omnipotent.

You are our Shepherd. You show
us how to live our life as you
intended for our happiness.

You are our Savior. Without
your paying the penalty for our
sins we would forever be apart
from you in sadness and suffering.

You alone know our hearts and
thoughts. Yet you love us so
much that you want us to spend
eternity with you. We cannot
fathom eternity nor where our
heavenly home will be.

Before you, our strength and pride
become weakness and humility.
Thus we worship you, we
praise you, and we love you.

TO MY MOTHER WHEN GONE TO WAR

by Brad Buchanan

Sing it to the birds,
My mother is gone.
Let them carry my song,
Moving as they do
From here to there
And back again.

She who stood with axe and shield
Between the world and her son,
Who bade me not sail if it not be my will
To foreign lands with daring friends.
But bound by oath, we never looked back;
Her love she tucked away in my pack
And knew we would meet again
In one world or another.

So sing it to the birds,
For those who have gone.
Let them carry our song,
Moving as they do
From here to there
And back again.

GALE

Charged with a consuming zeal.
Commanding,
authoritative
forceful,
dominating.
Yet he's gentle with a child.

Impassioned with a fervent need.
Assertive,
majestic,
imperious,
aggressive.
Yet he's gentle with a woman.

Note: This was written a few weeks before our marriage on June 18, 1970.

Carol's Obituary

MRS. EVA CAROL JONES BUCHANAN, 80

Mrs. Eva Carol Jones Buchanan, age 80, passed away Sunday, November 6, 2022, in Tallahassee, Florida.

She was born on May 24, 1942, in Montgomery, Alabama, to her parents, Dixie Nell Jones and James Ramsey Jones. She was retired as an administrator/secretary.

Carol loved music. She loved to sing and to write poetry. But most of all, she loved to help other people without any expectation of receiving something in return. To her, the reward was making someone's life better.

She had a quick wit and keen sense of humor and did not shy away from sharing her frequent and forthright opinions (the "correct" opinions). She was a master at *Reader's Digest* Word Power puzzles and often beat the *Jeopardy!* contestants on TV. Playing Scrabble on her iPad was one of her favorite pastimes.

Carol earned her associate of arts degree from Judson College and took courses at Auburn University, Abraham Baldwin Agricultural College, and Valdosta State University.

In retirement, she was an avid birdwatcher. She loved all songbirds but was especially fond of the northern cardinals that came to her window feeder.

While her stroke in 2015 slowed her down a bit physically, she still looked forward to each Sunday when she could visit with all of her church friends.

She is survived by her husband of fifty-two years, Gale Buchanan, of Adel, Georgia; one son, Brad Buchanan (Kymberly) of Adel, Georgia; one daughter, Judy B. Holmes (Sammy) of Birmingham, Alabama; one brother, James Ramsey Jones Jr. (Libby) of Mobile, Alabama; three sisters, Janet Jones (Louie Whitehead) of Daphne, Alabama, Cherry Duncan (Roy) of Mobile, Alabama, and Suzy Braswell of Mobile, Alabama; two grandchildren, Lachlan Buchanan and Stephen Holmes.

While flowers are welcome, memorial donations can be made to the Southeast Georgia Fellowship of Christian Athletes, 1709-A Gornto Road, Valdosta, GA 31601, or online in care of Mr. Bobby Willis at my.fca.org/bobbywillis.

Funeral services were 11:00 a.m., Saturday, November 12, 2022, at Hickory Grove Methodist Church, with burial at Hickory Grove Cemetery. Visitation was one hour prior to service at the church.

You may send condolences to the family by visiting our website at www.beggsfuneral.com.

About the Author

Gale Buchanan is the former undersecretary for Research, Education, and Economics and chief scientist for the US Department of Agriculture. He was also a former dean and director of the Alabama Agricultural Experiment Station—as well as dean and director emeritus of the College of Agricultural and Environmental Sciences at the University of Georgia. Gale was a graduate of both the University of Florida and Iowa State University where he earned the PhD.

While serving in academic assignments, he also served as a member of the US Army Reserves and the Alabama Army National Guard. He rose to the rank of colonel and retired from the Alabama Army National Guard after 34 years of service. Among his last assignments in the guard was commandant of the Alabama Military Academy.

This is Gale's sixth book. His most recent book, *Unexpected Chef* was published in 2023. All of his books may be purchased from amazon.com or barnesandnoble.com.

Gale's wife of over 52 years, Carol, died November 6, 2022. Today, Gale lives in Adel, Georgia and occasionally visits his farm near Pinetta, Florida.